SURVIVING THE
TECH
STORM

STRATEGY IN TIMES OF
TECHNOLOGICAL UNCERTAINTY

Published by
LID Publishing Ltd
One Adam Street, London. WC2N 6LE

31 West 34th Street, Suite 7004,
New York, NY 10001, US

info@lidpublishing.com
www.lidpublishing.com

A member of:

www.businesspublishersroundtable.com

© Nicklas Bergman 2016
© LID Publishing Inc., 2016
Techstorm™, Surviving the Techstorm™ and Techstorm 44™

Printed in Great Britain by TJ International
ISBN: 978-1-910649-19-0

Cover design: Laura Hawkins
Page design: Caroline Li

SURVIVING THE
TECH
STORM

STRATEGY IN TIMES OF
TECHNOLOGICAL UNCERTAINTY

NICKLAS BERGMAN

LONDON   MONTERREY
MADRID   SHANGHAI
MEXICO CITY   BOGOTA
NEW YORK   BUENOS AIRES
BARCELONA   SAN FRANCISCO

Dedication

To Anna, Valdemar, Inez and Beata,
my strongest supporters and fiercest critics…

CONTENTS

FOREWORD

Are we living, today, in a more exciting, dangerous, dismaying, encouraging time than any other in history? We really do not know, but we do know that each new era and technological paradigm shift presents particular challenges and opportunities. It is a constant struggle to keep up with the fast changing times in which we live, and it is only a minor comfort to realize that, during the 19th century, humankind already felt left behind and overwhelmed by information overload, globalization and technological progress. One of the main reasons people react in this way is that technological developments create opportunities and challenges, simultaneously this is questioning and challenging existing perceptions and behaviors.

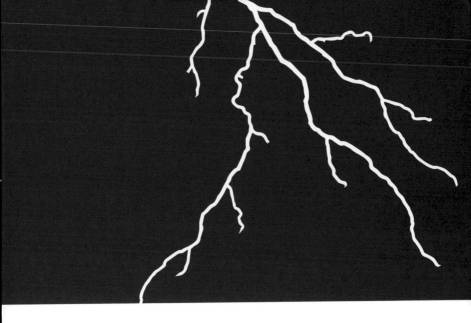

My grandmother, Selma Olsson, was born in 1900, and gave birth to 17 children between 1920 and 1944. Quite apart from that marvelous achievement, by the time she passed away in 1992, she had also experienced close to a century of amazing technological development. Among other things, she witnessed the mainstream adoption of the telephone and electricity, the arrival of radio and television, new means of transportation with cars and air travel, the conquering of space, as well as the invention of the computer. She lived her whole life in the countryside off the Swedish west coast, and although she was a curious and open minded person, she never really embraced all

My grandmother Selma Olsson, circa 1920.
Credit: Private

the new technologies, instead being very content with her way of living. The lives of my children, born at the beginning of the 21st century, could not be more different. We are entering an era in which technology will redefine who we are, and it is no longer just a question of what technology can do for us, but what should we allow technology to do.

For more than 20 years I have worked as an entrepreneur, technology investor and futurist, focusing mostly on investments and business development in emerging markets, web services, nanotechnology, computing, new materials and new media art. Currently, I have approximately 15 direct and indirect technology investments. The constant challenge is to choose a technological path and to time development and/or market introduction. This involves identifying key indicators that can be of help in these decision-making processes; often the companies or projects end up having to make major decisions based on very limited information.

Over the past 10 years, I have spent a significant amount of time and energy trying to gain some deeper understanding of the decisio-making processes under these complicated circumstances. This book is an attempt to create a framework for how we relate to these times of enormous technological turbulence. By combining a historical perspective with technological curiosity and strategic business insight, it is possible to gain a clear view of both the

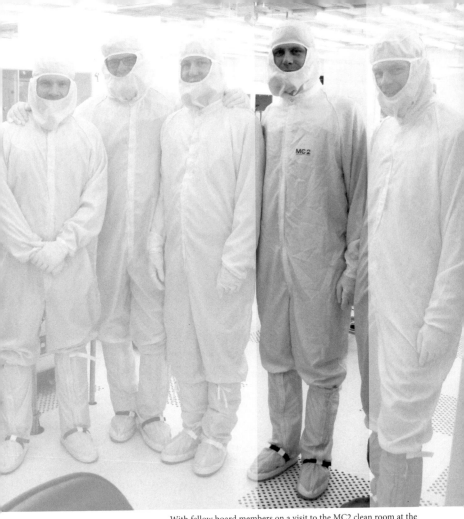

With fellow board members on a visit to the MC2 clean room at the
Chalmers University of Technology in Gothenburg, Sweden.
Credit: M Shafiq Kabir

opportunities and challenges coming out of the
approaching techstorm.

Enjoy the read, and please let me know if you
have any comments or suggestions. E-mail me
at write@nicklasbergman.com

Stockholm, November 2015

ACKNOWLEDGEMENTS

A book is definitely not a solo project and, although I am fully and solely responsible for everything in it, I have lots of people to thank for their help, insights, comments, and guidance.

First, thanks to Magnus Lindkvist for introducing me to LID Publishing, and thanks to Martin Liu, Sara Taheri, Caroline Li, Niki Mullin, Amrita Brard, and Tasneem Mahmoud at LID Publishing for taking care of me during this whole project. I really look forward to continuing working with you guys.

Thanks to Anders Bergkvist, Hugh Courtney, Niklas Hagberg, Pia Irell, Jakob Lindberg, and David Stiernholm for bouncing ideas and being

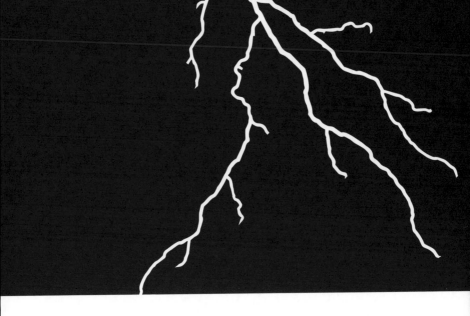

patient early in the process when I tried to visualize my ideas. Also thanks to Yury Boshyk, Scott Bourke, Brian David Johnson, Anne-Lise Kjaer, Ramez Naam, Andreas Uhr, and Amy Zalman for your input and giving me a different perspective on the future.

Thanks to Lars-Johan Jarnheimer at IKEA, Martin Lorentzon and Angela Woods at Spotify, Thomas Mattsson at Expressen, and Stephen Wolfram at Wolfram Research for the interviews and help with case material.

Thanks to Dag Wetterberg and Pauline Riccius for helping me understand the publishing industry.

Also, thanks to Valdemar, Inez, and Beata for accepting that your dad has been physically and mentally unavailable for long periods of time. Finally, thanks to my wife Anna for her strong support and for being a great discussion partner in all parts of the book project – you are the best!

MEGATRENDS AS DRIVERS OF CHANGE

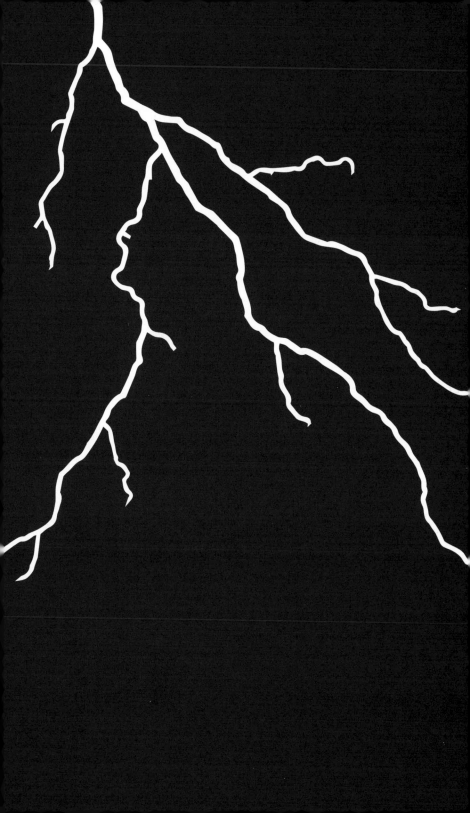

Over the next 50 years, society will need to respond to myriad issues relating to the proper use and consequences of unprecedented developments, and the insights these provide. With every technological advance mankind makes, there are potentially thousands of questions that will be generated, the majority concerning the appropriate uses and application of that technology and determining whether the benefits are worth the price the planet ends up paying. In the coming years and decades, it will no longer be a question of what technology can do for us, but rather what we should allow technology to do. It will be increasingly important that society, taking account of individual beliefs as well as joint values, discusses and agrees on our technological future. It's an ongoing revolution, and we have to take control.

In the coming years and decades, it will no longer be a question of what technology can do for us, but rather what we should allow technology to do.

Technological development is the most powerful of all megatrends, and the one that often fuels development in others; a healthier population, with people living longer; the global environmental challenge; a more global and connected

MEGATRENDS

TECHNOLOGIES

CASES

FRAMEWORK

EXECUTION

TECHSTORM 44

world and a power shift in the global economy. The goal must always be to understand the megatrends of today, to gain insight into the different societal and technological, but also ethical, dimensions that come from innovations, new systems and practices. The ultimate goal is not to destroy technology and remove it from society, but rather to help with the advancement of a technological society that does not sacrifice morals and ethics for the sake of having the technology. Megatrends bring significant changes that affect society in powerful ways and the goal of those who study these trends is to understand the potential impacts.

HEALTHIER AND OLDER DEMOGRAPHY

There is no doubt that technology is developing very rapidly, faster than most people know how to make use of it. The technological revolution we are facing today makes it all the more vital and necessary for people to understand the impact megatrends have on the world as a whole. The demography of cities, regions and countries changes all the time and these developments are largely influenced by the societal changes and advancements that are made. Demography is more than just the data and numbers of who is

Demography is more than just the data and numbers of who is who in a given area, it is about understanding what happens to them and why.

MEGATRENDS AS DRIVERS OF CHANGE

MEGATRENDS

TECHNOLOGIES

CASES

FRAMEWORK

EXECUTION

TECHSTORM 44

who in a given area, it is about understanding what happens to them and why. The way people live, work, and develop as a society is the basis for the study of this megatrend; it is virtually impossible to separate changing demographic patterns from the other megatrends.

In the areas of demographics and technology, there are four key developments that need to be addressed: Ageing; improving standards of health; empowering individuals and harnessing their power; and recognizing trends and developments and keeping a watchful eye on what the future holds.

AGEING POPULATION

"The so called 'baby boom' generation (people born between 1946 and 1964) is already having an effect on the healthcare system and this is expected to increase as the century progresses. The number of American citizens aged 65 and over (35 million people in 2000) will rise by more than 19 million to 54 million by 2020. From 2000 to 2050, the number of people aged 65 and older will increase from 12.5% to 20% of the US population."[1] In the US, more than 10 000 people celebrates their fiftieth birthday every day. Proportionally, the size of the older population is growing at a faster rate than the younger population. In Japan, the number of people who are aged 75 and over has grown by almost 40% between 2005 and 2015.

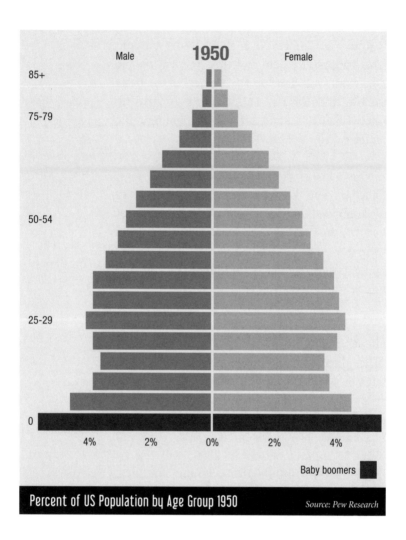

1950

Male   Female

85+

75-79

50-54

25-29

0

4%   2%   0%   2%   4%

Baby boomers

Percent of US Population by Age Group 1950   *Source: Pew Research*

Trends like these are the same across the globe and bring to light a fact that cannot be ignored: the world's population is aging. That brings a whole new list of issues that must be addressed and dealt with.

The impact of this shift in population demographics is far reaching and spans many industries.

MEGATRENDS AS DRIVERS OF CHANGE

MEGATRENDS

TECHNOLOGIES

CASES

FRAMEWORK

EXECUTION

TECHSTORM 44

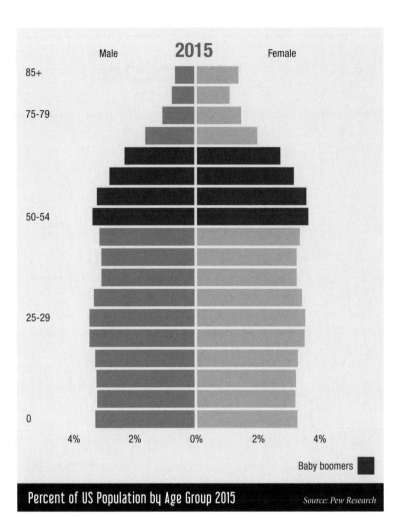

Percent of US Population by Age Group 2015   *Source: Pew Research*

Aging populations affect all areas of health and social care, and the impact is felt not only by the older population itself, but by the coming generations who must help to support and care for them. Medical advances have been made and new medicines and treatments are being developed, but the needs of the ageing population are also growing at a rapid rate.[2]

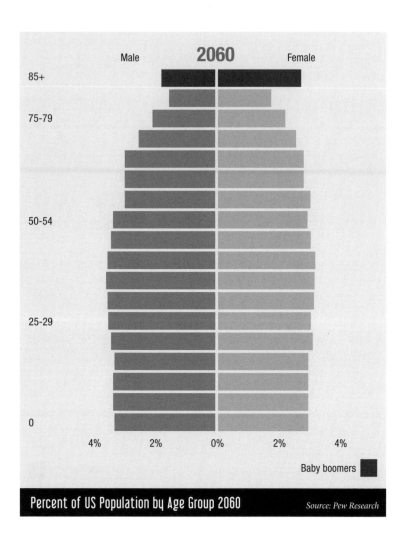

2060

Male   Female

Percent of US Population by Age Group 2060   *Source: Pew Research*

Since diseases such as dementia, diabetes, cancer, age-related health problems and other chronic conditions become more prevalent as people live longer, the burden that is placed on the healthcare industry, as well as all members of society, increases.

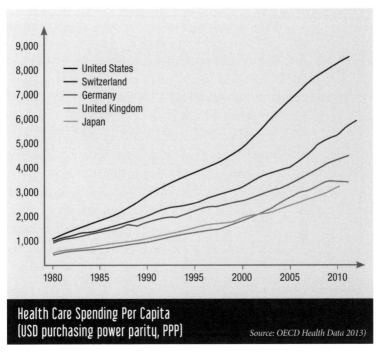

Health Care Spending Per Capita
(USD purchasing power parity, PPP)   *Source: OECD Health Data 2013)*

IMPROVING HEALTH

"The $414.3 billion in healthcare expenses for the elderly in 2011 was over $100 billion higher than inflation adjusted expenses for 2001. ... The average annual [medical] expense per person was about $1,000 higher in 2011 than 2001."[3] This data comes from the US, and although the country has the highest healthcare spending per capita in the world[4], figures like these are showing up time and time again in surveys, medical studies and reports from many other countries. It is little wonder that the aging population of the world struggles to get the care they need to have full and valuable lives.

Up until quite recently, at least from a history of humanity perspective, famine, pestilence, war and natural disaster were control mechanisms limiting population growth. Lower birth survival rates and higher death rates slowed the population increase. With recent advances in medicine, this is no longer the case and as populations swell, communities are facing the challenge of both supporting the young, the working population and older people, in need of care, for longer and longer periods of time. This put enormous stress on the welfare system, and is one of the most pressing issues concerning politicians today.[5]

The Millennium Project, along with many others like it, measures the guiding principles that are thought to be the most influential in shaping, for example, ethical decision-making, both now and in the future.

THE POWER OF ONE

Our understanding of how to use technology and the way technology impacts society will change year on year. What's "right" today may not be "right" five years from now. However, there are certain constants that seem likely always to play a factor in determining how technology should be used.[6]

This applies to the concept that has come to be called "the power of one" because it focuses on how an individual's needs, goals, and actions can lead to bigger advances. Every person can create a ripple effect in an interconnected world. The power of one focuses on the change that happens in a society where trends, fads, and acceptable norms are in flux; there is a constant ebb and flow that helps govern societies and dictate accepted norms and values. There is still power in the individual and even one person can make a difference. A few united minds can be enough to fuel serious change and revolutions. The Millennium Project, along with many others like it, measures the guiding principles that are thought to be the most influential in shaping, for example, ethical decision-making, both now and in the future. What many similar studies have uncovered is that the needs and values of a population are not continuous but fluid. Some of the most important values and needs of today will not be considered important in a few decades. Examples are changes in societal norms, changes in the needs and desires of the population, changes in health and lifespans, current events that shape the way groups view the world, and the ever changing interests and convictions of individuals.

TRENDS IN DEMOGRAPHIC ETHICS

While these principles do not directly explain how megatrends impact society, or how these advances and changes should be used, they are elements that are generally agreed upon in the process of making ethical decisions. Technology usage and social norms that potentially threaten human survival, for example, do not fit into ethical usage. Society will have to adjust its views on certain topics and issues involved.[7] While it is true that changes in demographic trends mean there is a greater demand for resources, supplies, money, healthcare, and so on, this does not mean that the world is doomed to a future of scarcity and an everyday battle for basic necessities. What it does mean is that there must be a shift in how people see and approach these trends and how society adheres to these changes. Demographic trends are connected to every aspect of society, including, but not limited to, environment, culture, job markets, and financial stability.

MEGATRENDS AS DRIVERS OF CHANGE

MEGATRENDS

TECHNOLOGIES

CASES

FRAMEWORK

EXECUTION

TECHSTORM 44

URGENT BUT HOPEFUL - ENVIRONMENT

"Rising greenhouse gas emissions are causing climate change and driving a complex mix of unpredictable changes to the environment while further taxing the resilience of natural and built systems. Achieving the right combination of adaptation and mitigation policies will be difficult for most governments."[8] This is just one example of the growing need for a renewed focus on global climate change and environmental impacts as they relate to megatrends. While many advances have happened, thanks to technology, many problems and concerns have also been created by the technological advances we enjoy today. There are various key areas that must be addressed when it comes to the environmental: the environment as a whole; environmental decline; food, water and energy concerns; unsustainable growth; scarcity versus abundance of resources; and the impact of climate change.

THE BIG PICTURE - THE ENVIRONMENT

One thing that will always remain, regardless of the advances that technology brings to us, is that we rely on planet Earth to sustain us. Despite the fact that our lives have been made easier, we have to consider the impact we are having on the planet. We can no longer ignore the damage that has been, and is being, done to the planet and the ripple effect it has on every aspect of life on Earth. This is one of the main reasons why there has been such a push towards sustainable and environmentally friendly practices during the past decade.

"Important features of the sustainable and competitive city will be features that are 'green' and 'smart'. Green cities will have energy efficient buildings, reduced waste and rely heavily on renewable energy sources and energy efficient transportation systems. Enabled by digital technology, competitive cities will also make use of state-of-the-art information and communication technology (ICT) to build smart mobility solutions, smart grids and other solutions."[9] No longer can the scientific facts be ignored or brushed off simply because they are inconvenient. Change has to happen and a new and renewed commitment to protecting the environment is a major focus of countless studies that look at the power and impact of megatrends.

ENVIRONMENTAL DECLINE AND LOSS

An important set of tasks in today's world is to research, understand, measure, and report how

MEGATRENDS AS DRIVERS OF CHANGE

MEGATRENDS

TECHNOLOGIES

CASES

FRAMEWORK

EXECUTION

TECHSTORM 44

the actions and decisions that society makes affect the environment. This needs to be done by individuals, businesses, societies, and entire countries. Over time, progress in the area of environmental protection, renewal, and innovation will "help businesses understand and explain their impacts more fully, make better informed decisions, and rebuild public trust by providing wider and more credible insights."[10]

A similar debate that is coming to light concerns how far one group can go in order to empower itself or others. How far is too far when it comes to protecting the environment? Should environmental concerns surpass concern for individuals, groups, and societies? Some would argue that every group is responsible for its own success or failure. Others see the global community as one open system within which every group gives and takes and helps either build up or tear down the structure. Whether from the viewpoint of science or the moral viewpoint of the human mind, the Earth can be seen either as a closed system or an open system. That has a huge impact on the way people make decisions and view the changes in the world around them.[11]

THE FOOD, WATER, AND ENERGY SITUATION

"During the 21st century, global warming is projected to continue and climate changes are likely to intensify. Scientists have used climate models to project different aspects of future climate, including temperature, precipitation, snow and ice, ocean level, and ocean acidity. Depending

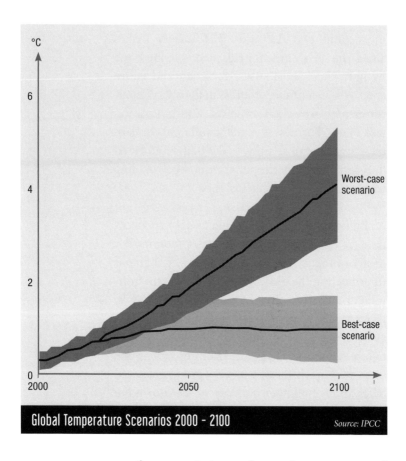

°C

6

4

2

Worst-case
scenario

Best-case
scenario

0
2000   2050   2100

Global Temperature Scenarios 2000 - 2100   *Source: IPCC*

on future emissions of greenhouse gases and
how the climate responds, average global tem-
peratures are projected to increase worldwide by
2°F to 11.5°F [1°C to 6°C] by 2100."[12] There is no
doubt that the world's climate, though known to
go through natural changes and cycles, is now
changing at a rapid, unnatural pace, and the
absolute majority of indicators point to the bulk
of that change being attributable to mankind.

MEGATRENDS AS DRIVERS OF CHANGE

MEGATRENDS

TECHNOLOGIES

CASES

FRAMEWORK

EXECUTION

TECHSTORM 44

UNSUSTAINABLE ECONOMIC GROWTH

The effects of climate change, such as changes in weather patterns, rising sea levels, and increases in the frequency of super storms and natural disasters, will hit some areas of the world harder than others. Some results of unsustainable growth include lack of water and food, pollution and contamination concerns, increasing illnesses and diseases, and lower standards of living. Some issues are felt more in larger cities and more congested population areas while others seem to be more closely tied to rural areas. The World Health Organization (WHO) reported that seven million people died as a result of air pollution exposure in 2012, a large proportion of these individuals were residing in urban areas.[13]

While pollution may not be as much of an issue in rural areas, the lack of resources needed to sustain important industries such as farming, forestry, mining, and so forth is a huge issue that impacts the lives of people living in these areas. Rural communities rely on natural resources for many of the jobs that supply income to their residents; when natural resources cannot be sustained at an appropriate level, the entire community suffers. Farms close, materials become scarce, prices go up, and the job market and economy suffer. This is one area that many do not fully understand when they begin examining the environmental megatrends of today, because of the separation that still exists between urban and rural areas.

RESOURCES: SCARCE AND ABUNDANT

"Absolute population growth, economic development and more middle class consumers will drive increasing global demand for natural resources – both renewable and non-renewable. While the world's supply of non-renewable resources is technically finite, new technologies continue to impact the future supply picture by allowing access to formerly hard-to-reach and valuable oil, gas, and strategic mineral reserves. The application of new technologies, as well as the shifting supply environment, will drive business model adaptation and innovation in multiple sectors – as well as impact the geopolitical balance of power."[14]

Technological developments help to shape the world in which we live; in fact, many of the advances we have seen in recent years have made it easier to attain the natural resources we need. One of the biggest issues that people face when looking at environmental megatrends

Absolute population growth, economic development and more middle class consumers will drive increasing global demand for natural resources – both renewable and non-renewable.

is recognizing that without the technology we have today, we would not have access to resources such as oil and natural gases and that it would be much more difficult and costly to acquire resources such as wood and ore to generate energy.

IMPACT OF CLIMATE CHANGE

It is impossible to ignore the reports that show, year on year, the increase in greenhouse gas emissions and the devastating effects they are having on the environment. While it is true that the world has gone through cycles of warming and cooling throughout its history, the concern with current trends is that they are happening faster, and going further, than ever before. Though the world's population at one time remained fairly balanced, this is no longer the case; populations around the world continue to swell. And although there is a scientific consensus that Earth's population will level off around 11 billion[15], the planet is struggling to support a growing population. Almost two-thirds of the world's population will live in big cities by the year 2050.[16] The growth of the human population and the resulting climate changes makes it vital for technology to assist in developing a plan for more sustainable living and protecting the balance of the global population, infrastructure and resources.[17] With more people alive on the earth today than have lived in its entire existence up until now, there is strain on the planet unlike anything that has been seen before.

BOTH PHYSICAL AND MENTAL – GLOBALIZATION

In the ever-changing world in which we live, there is a trend that is building up speed at an alarming rate. It is one that cannot be stopped and shows no signs of slowing down. This is the trend of globalization and the changing landscape of the journey each and every person takes. "We are all time travellers on a journey into the future ... Our fellow explorers express many different opinions about what lies ahead. Some of them foresee a marvelous paradise – a time filled with wonderful new technologies that will keep us all well fed, healthy, and happy. Others among us warn of doom in one form or another: an ecological catastrophe, a new Ice Age, a collision with a comet, or any of an endless variety of other threats, some more plausible than others."[18] It is this dichotomy of views that fuels the debate about globalization and the impact it has on the world.

MEGATRENDS AS DRIVERS OF CHANGE

MEGATRENDS

TECHNOLOGIES

CASES

FRAMEWORK

EXECUTION

TECHSTORM 44

GLOBAL CONNECTIVITY

In an era of lightning-fast communications over the internet, via cell phones, computers, and wireless devices, mankind has the lowest levels of interaction and socialization ever seen, but do not forget that other forms of being antisocial existed in the 20th century.

"It is one of the more ironic consequences of digitization that the more connected we become, the more isolated we feel. Part of the reason for this is that most of our new found connectivity is wafer thin. We have traded intimacy for familiarity and we are now paying the price."[19] That said, in a globalized, connected world where we actually have access to all information, in an instant, wherever we are and, at least in theory, can reach out to people all over the world and receive an immediate response, a positive sense of belonging is sure to emerge for anyone that understands.

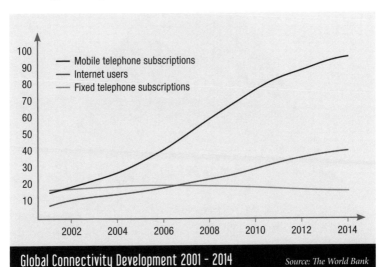

Global Connectivity Development 2001 - 2014   *Source: The World Bank*

For all the advances that have made us live longer, work smarter, grow richer, and have more things than we have ever had before, are we really better off? Are we happy? No one has yet been able to answer that question because it is a personal one, with as many answers as there are people pondering the question. Although, if you look at the developed world, almost everyone has managed his or her basic physiological and safety needs. The next step is, then, the search for belonging, esteem and self actualization, and this is where today's challenges begin. These needs are psychological, often vague by nature, and personal in the sense that it is mostly up to the individual to reach them.

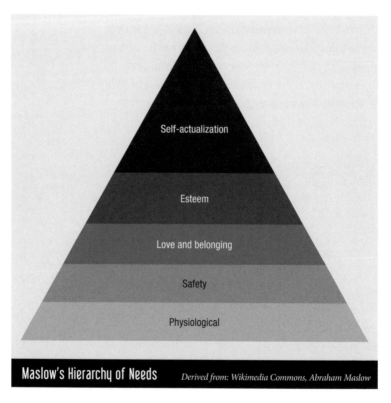

Maslow's Hierarchy of Needs   *Derived from: Wikimedia Commons, Abraham Maslow*

MEGATRENDS AS DRIVERS OF CHANGE

MEGATRENDS

TECHNOLOGIES

CASES

FRAMEWORK

EXECUTION

TECHSTORM 44

INCREASED MOBILITY

One of the most far-reaching effects of a globalized and digitized world is the increase in mobility attained by much of the population. Global travel can now take a matter of hours, instead of weeks or months. We can get from one place to another with relative ease thanks to automobiles, trains, boats, and planes. If used right, this is a tremendous source of inspiration and adventure.

However, with that increased ease of travel has come an unexpected downside. As people travel the globe for business and pleasure, they also bring and take away with them a range of problems, from diseases to new ideas and temptations. Some cultures have been very guarded and protected over the centuries and now, in a world that is mobile and connected, that isolation is gone.

However, despite the increased mobility in terms of travel and transportation, people today are very much stationary when it comes to getting out of their comfort zones. They may travel the world for their jobs, but they never enjoy it and never appreciate its full potential. People who are able to break the mold and step off the mundane path of mobility without connection can experience and achieve great things. "This can be daunting because it includes an element of risk and necessitates people stepping out of their comfort zones. The people who do this successfully are able to make a tremendous positive impact and find even more opportunities to make a difference... It is possible to be successful... but true differentiation… is achievable only for those who are willing to dive into new areas."[20]

GLOBAL COMMUNICATIONS

The pressures of population growth, economic turbulence, and climate change have grown and continue to place increased strain on the natural resources and reserves that are essential to human survival, including water, food, land, and energy. These issues make sustainable resource management a necessity and a focus of government plans and preparations. But with this dire need also comes the necessity to communicate at a global level. And despite the advances, there is one thing that mankind has not mastered yet – setting aside differences and working towards the betterment of all groups, not just one. When different cultures, countries, and peoples are connected, they become dependent on one another for their economic stability and the buying and selling of goods. There is an essential need for clear communications and the ability to

In today's world, where the circles of business, personal life, global cultural exchange, and income continue to overlap, there are many good examples of how people overcome political, religious and cultural differences to cooperate, trade and solve common challenges.

MEGATRENDS

TECHNOLOGIES

CASES

FRAMEWORK

EXECUTION

TECHSTORM 44

overcome differences and deal with conflicts and disagreements. In today's world, where the circles of business, personal life, global cultural exchange, and income continue to overlap, there are many good examples of how people overcome political, religious and cultural differences to cooperate, trade and solve common challenges. Of course, there are still enormous challenges out there, but only through communication and interaction becoming part of the solution; we will find a way forward.

A SPLINTERED WORLD

Achieving the right combination of adaptation and mitigation policies is difficult for most governments. "The complexity and uncertainty associated with climate change often paralyzes government action at national and international levels. However, combating climate change will require unprecedented levels of multilateral cooperation to prevent the worst effects of rising CO_2 levels in the next century. This will also require immediate efforts to 'climate proof' communities for the effects of climate change that are already locked in."[21] The biggest challenge in dealing with megatrends and the impact they have on the world at large is not in figuring out what needs to be done. In many cases it is clear what is needed to find common grounds and ways to move forward. The difficulty comes in getting different groups to band together, see eye-to-eye and work toward a common goal while putting aside their differences.

GLOBALIZATION AND LOSS OF CULTURES

What does the future hold for the many varied cultures and groups that are spread throughout the world? Cultures have risen and fallen throughout human history and that continues today, but which ones will last and which ones will fade? Which cultures will stand on their own and which will fall or disappear into the pages of history as new powers rise? No one has a crystal ball. But we can know enough about the future that we can plan. There is a difference between prediction and foresight. Prediction is trying to divine the precise future – an impossible task. Foresight understands the factors or variables that can, or may, produce the future. Inevitably, foresight talks about alternative futures – because how we shape those trends can lead to different futures."[22]

Traditions are changing, culture is altered, and societal views are warped. This is one of the effects of a globalized world and one of the issues that are brought about because of the growth and reach of the globalization megatrend. Is it worth technological advances and an "easier life" if cultures lose their traditions and if groups stop being unique and diversified? Should cultures give up their practices and rituals just to fit in with a united global community? Will we see new and interesting cultural phenomena based on a mix of different influences (Gangnam style, anyone?)? Those are just some of the questions that the megatrend of globalization in the modern age has brought up to be answered.

MEGATRENDS AS DRIVERS OF CHANGE

MEGATRENDS

TECHNOLOGIES

CASES

FRAMEWORK

EXECUTION

TECHSTORM 44

GLOBAL GROWTH AND POWER SHIFT – ECONOMICS

"Science and, to a lesser extent, technology have always operated within a political context, but until recently they were more or less left alone. Not anymore though; both will come under the microscope as society debates not whether something is possible but whether its consequences are desirable. Top of the list of gatekeepers will be the government, with its own national and international agenda based on political philosophy, the economy and defense." [23]

ECONOMIC GROWTH AND EMPOWERING INDIVIDUALS

"Globalization is a process of interaction and integration among the people, companies, and governments of different nations; it is a process driven by international trade and investment and aided by information technology. This process has effects on the environment, on culture, on political systems, on economic development and prosperity, and on human physical well-being in societies around the world."[24] The idea and general concept of globalization, however, is far from new. For many thousands of years, local, regional, and later, transcontinental and intercontinental trade has been one of the corner stones in economic development.

Famous trade routes such as the Silk Road of central Asia and spice routes of India make it obvious that extended systems of buying and selling have long been a part of human civilization. Also, the East India Companies that were incorporated in Europe, starting in the 17th century, created new entities limiting

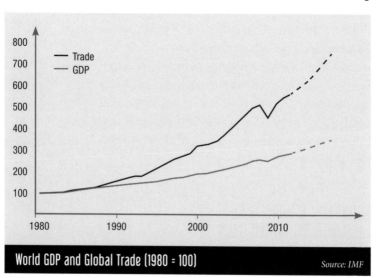

World GDP and Global Trade (1980 = 100)   *Source: IMF*

individual exposure to risk. During the 20th century, global trade has exploded, and is today one of the fundamental drivers of economic growth and globalization.

SEPARATED, YET UNITED AND VULNERABLE YET STRONG

What is interesting when one looks closely at the megatrend of globalization and associated economic trends is the strange and somewhat twisted dichotomy of the modern world. People today are separated by the differences in the technology to which they have access while at the same time having the potential to be more connected than in all of human history. Mankind is vulnerable due to fear of change, while at the same time, remaining strong and determined to preserve our race. "Only a reckless fool would imagine that problems will sit patiently waiting until we find it convenient to receive them ... problems may rush upon us at the worst possible moment, and our very survival could depend on how well we have prepared for them."[25] The times, people, and the world are changing constantly and research is pointing out, time and again, that preparation is critical to the sustainability of modern society.

A lack of preparation and a disregard for the warning signs that are evident, does nothing but invite disaster. Many people today would rather stick their heads in the sand, ignore the signs and pretend that there is nothing to worry about. It is widely accepted now that many developing

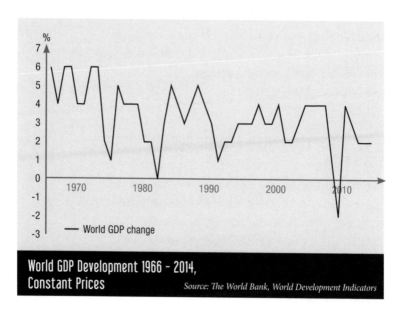

World GDP Development 1966 - 2014, Constant Prices *Source: The World Bank, World Development Indicators*

countries are not benefiting as much as they could, or should, from global economic growth. The reason for this is often that globalization and new technologies are being initiated from, and formed with, an already developed society in mind, meaning that it is based on and intro-duced into an environment where basic systems and infrastructure are already in place. Everyone that benefits from the current technological and economic environment has a responsibility to make sure that the result of their actions are not harmful to others and, more specifically, those less fortunate than themselves.

CONCLUSION - LOOKING TO THE FUTURE

Ultimately, all the megatrends are changing our world at a rapid rate. From political and social structures as a response to the fears about the future[26], the changes in migratory patterns as a response to military conflicts, changes in climate, temperature, and habitat availability[27], or the crisis of dwindling food, water, and natural resources[28], the planet, and all the creatures living on it, including mankind, are struggling to adapt and survive. In the coming years, society will be tasked with finding an answer to lots of questions relating to the proper use of the technological advances and new abilities mankind has granted itself. With each and every advance mankind makes with new technology, there will be thousands of potential dilemmas, side effects, and questions that will need to be answered. Most of them will deal with the appropriate uses and application of these new technologies and will focus on determining whether the benefits are worth the price the planet ends up paying.

"The megatrends illustrate a world in motion. Economic power continues to shift eastward. New markets and new trade linkages are emerging. The boundaries between industry sectors are blurring. New entrants who are digitally native are overturning existing business models. Existing players in one sector (technology) are entering other sectors (health) with exciting new propositions. As we hurtle towards 2030, developments within these ... megatrends, as well as the interplay between them, will certainly bear close watching."[29] We see a power shift where economic turmoil, slow growth and political indecision inhibit Europe, where Russia is alienating itself, and despite China's relative growth slow down, a look east and south shows regions of high growth, interesting innovations and exciting market opportunities.

The megatrends that are shaping our world offer important insights and direction that sheds light on the mystery of where we are going as the human race. Sometimes, the outlook is grim and other times it is promising; what the reality ends up being depends largely on mankind's ability to adapt, adjust, and plan for a better future. The rapid acceleration of knowledge and the mind-blowing advances of technology leave the future up to mankind as a whole to determine the course taken and the future we, as a species, choose to walk towards, or in some cases, run. The role of research and study is to help mankind get there in the best shape possible while fully understanding the short term and long term impact these megatrends have on all of human civilization.

The megatrends that are shaping our world offer important insights and direction that sheds light on the mystery of where we are going as the human race.

BROADEN YOUR TECHNOLOGY PERSPECTIVE

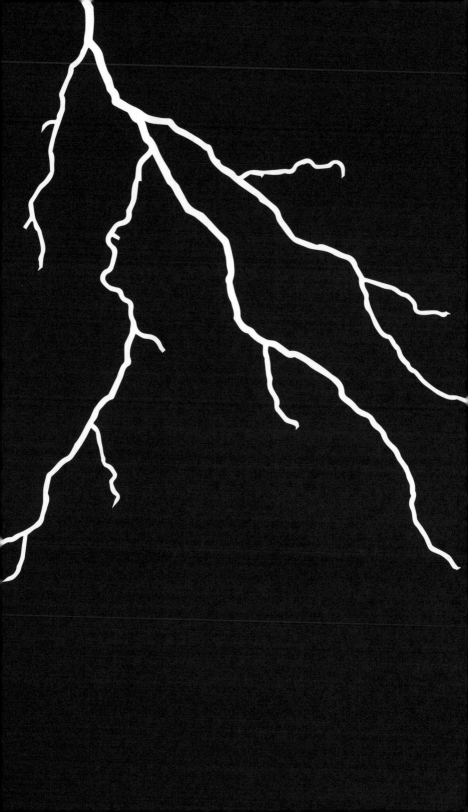

THE HISTORY OF TECHNOLOGY

Throughout history, major changes in society and the way people live and do business have been determined by the developments in technology corresponding to each particular era.

Over the past 300 years, the world has changed dramatically. Today it would barely be recognizable to someone from the 18th century. What has made the world so different? From the way people live to the way they do business, almost everything about existence has been impacted by five distinct waves of technological innovation.

These technology waves[30] have resulted in progression in society, with each wave inciting change and advancement before eventually giving way to a new wave. In order to comprehend this, we must first look at the underlying technologies that make a technology wave possible.

MEGATRENDS

TECHNOLOGIES

CASES

FRAMEWORK

EXECUTION

TECHSTORM 44

THE IMPORTANCE OF GENERAL PURPOSE TECHNOLOGIES

None of the technology waves would have been possible without general-purpose technologies (GPT). GPTs are an essential component in connecting the past with the present and future technological outlooks. In general terms, a GPT is a single generic technology that develops over time but can still be recognized as the same technology over its lifetime. Initially, a GPT has much room for growth, and it eventually becomes widely used. It is not only used by many, but has numerous uses, and spills over into countless other areas and sectors. The wheel, the printing press and the computer are three great examples of GPTs that have paved the way for human advancement in many different areas.

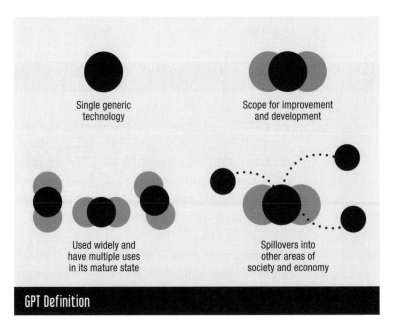

Single generic technology

Scope for improvement and development

Used widely and have multiple uses in its mature state

Spillovers into other areas of society and economy

GPT Definition

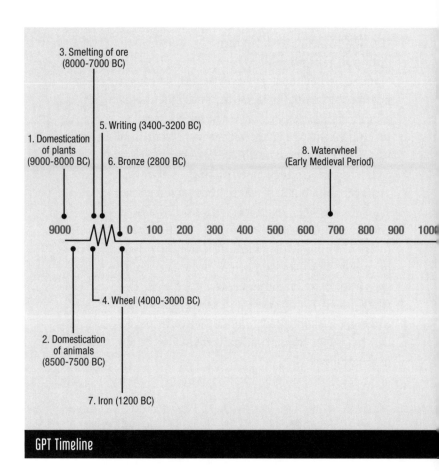

GPT Timeline

In order to have a new technological wave, there must be one, or several, GPTs to drive it. Identifying a GPT in its nascent state is very hard. However, there are many new technologies that can be labeled as potential GPTs, and to qualify, a technology must meet certain criteria.

Although many non-GPTs may have some of these characteristics, and may even demonstrate a single characteristic to a greater extent than a GPT, only a true GPT will have all four and will

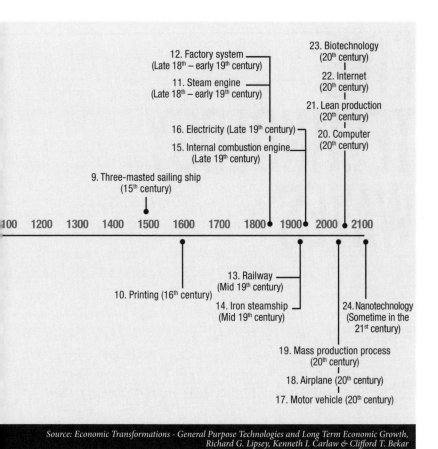

Source: *Economic Transformations - General Purpose Technologies and Long Term Economic Growth, Richard G. Lipsey, Kenneth I. Carlaw & Clifford T. Bekar*

be able to launch a new technological wave. For example, although gunpowder transformed the Western world in certain ways, it is not a GPT because of its limited use, and therefore it is not the centre point of a technological wave.

There is no doubt that the sixth technological wave is upon us, but before we can understand what is coming, it's important to look back at the first five waves and how they were shaped.

FIVE TECHNOLOGY WAVES

Human progress since the dawn of industrialization in the 1770s can be clearly divided into waves, based on periods of major transformation. A fresh wave, or a "successive industrial revolution", is initiated by new technology rather than just the growth of a specific industry.[32] Each wave is generally fuelled by one or several new GPTs, and as this technology develops and matures, an almost unrecognizable society forms in response.

EARLY MECHANIZATION (1770s TO 1830s)

Industrialization began in the UK near the end of the eighteenth century, revolving primarily around improvements in the textile industry. A money economy was already in place thanks to explorers and trade companies bringing precious metals and goods to the country, fuelling trade, and the emergence of a merchant class. As indi-

BROADEN YOUR TECHNOLOGY PERSPECTIVE

MEGATRENDS

TECHNOLOGIES

CASES

FRAMEWORK

EXECUTION

TECHSTORM 44

viduals began to amass wealth, they also began to want increasing quantities of better quality goods. With more efficient chemical processing and machinery like the spinning Jenny, the first automated weaving machine that started to replace hand tools, substantial growth and improvement in industry and quality became possible. Hand tools had long been a limitation in terms of production and quality, and the new technology of the first wave provided innovative solutions that allowed organized industry to grow.

This first technological wave centered on the spinning Jenny, which was able to meet the rising demands for cotton. Invented by James Hargreaves, this technology was necessary in order to speed up the processes of the textile industry. The spinning Jenny was an improvement on the previous technology of the flying shuttle, which had already nearly doubled productivity. Rather than only being able to work on one spool at a time, the spinning Jenny allowed workers to work on eight or more spools simultaneously. As the technology improved, this number eventually grew to more than 100 spools, creating a massive increase in productivity and availability. The spinning Jenny did much more than simply allow workers to produce more in less time. It also had significant implications for the economy and society as a whole. The ability to meet rising demand quickly started a chain reaction in the way work was organized.

During the first technological wave, there was also a major shift from a world that relied heavily on ships for trade. The mechanization of manufacturing and the development of factory towns went hand in hand with an increase in the need for transportation by land. Meanwhile, greater investment in machinery led to the organization of work by company and factory.

> The key technology during this wave was the railway, which gave society the ability to take full advantage of the steam engine.

Quality and productivity advances in agriculture, starting in the eighteenth century, followed by transportation improvements (mainly better roads and canal networks during the nineteenth century) lowered the cost of food. This, in turn, resulted in an increase in the UK population[33], coupled with a rapid expansion of the labour force. This first industrial wave ended when prices, wages, and profits all fell as a result of too much expansion and sent the early-industrialized nations into a major recession lasting until the mid-1840s.[34]

STEAM POWER AND RAILWAYS (1830s TO 1880s)

Although development of steam engines and steam power had already started during the first technology wave, the second wave thrived as a result of the improvements in these technologies.

MEGATRENDS

TECHNOLOGIES

CASES

FRAMEWORK

EXECUTION

TECHSTORM 44

While water and wind had been the primary sources of energy before this era, new steam engines began to take over during the second wave. Key to this development was an increase in efficiency, as newer steam engines meant coal consumption decreased from 30 to five pounds per horsepower hour.[35] As this technology became more efficient, it was applied in a variety of uses, including powering ships, railways, and factories.

The key technology during this wave was the railway, which gave society the ability to take full advantage of the steam engine. Economies were able to expand into new geographical territories by decentralized production and more efficient transportation. During the second technology wave, the US experienced some of the most rapid growth due to westward expansion and settlement, as well as the development of an enormous private railroad system across the nation.[36]

European economies enjoyed similar growth thanks to steam-driven locomotives. The UK's Liverpool to Manchester line opened for business in 1830 and provided passenger as well as freight services. This allowed for a massive industry expansion due mainly to larger addressable markets. The increase in labour demand from the first wave intensified, with some companies now needing thousands of employees. Competition increased, prices fell, and the financial sector swelled. There were also a lot more investment opportunities for the growing middle class, including limited liability and joint stock companies that developed in response to the new risks involved with larger corporations.[37]

ELECTRICAL AND HEAVY ENGINEERING (1880s TO 1930s)

The baton was taken up by the US. The third technology wave came about thanks to electricity, the combustion engine, and innovations concerning the processing of heavy chemicals. These key technologies led to the development of automobiles, aircraft, telecommunications, oils, and plastics. Manufacturing and construction overcame previous limitations in strength and durability with new inventions, making production processes cheaper.

As society began to understand how to harness, use, and distribute electricity, many technological breakthroughs became possible. Electrical power enabled the development of more efficient factories, allowing industry to expand further than it had during the second technology wave.

During these five decades, steam power was largely dropped in favor of electricity, which allowed for higher productivity and more efficient use of resources. The supply and distribution of electrical power also led to more flexible working hours, with people no longer dependent on daylight to get a job done. With increased efficiency and lower costs, businesses grew into giant firms. Monopolies formed and led to tighter government regulations. An example of this in the US was the Sherman Antitrust Act of 1890. This wave also saw the birth of new

BROADEN YOUR TECHNOLOGY PERSPECTIVE

MEGATRENDS

TECHNOLOGIES

CASES

FRAMEWORK

EXECUTION

TECHSTORM 44

organizational theories with more specialization and hierarchy, and as a consequence, a new type of role – middle management – a much needed management level as companies continued to grow in size. The third wave ended in the early stages of the US Great Depression, resulting in a 15% decline in worldwide gross domestic product (GDP) between 1929 and 1932.[38] The igniting factor was the crash of the US stock market, on October 29, 1929, known as "Black Tuesday", which prompted mass unemployment.

FORDIST MASS PRODUCTION (1930s TO 1970s)

The fourth technological wave began with arguably the most infamous and widespread economic depression the world has known. In spite of the Great Depression, the automobile continued to develop. There is little doubt that the automobile is what shaped this wave. It not only changed society by making it more mobile, but it changed industry and competition as a whole.

The need to meet the rising demand for cars led to mass production and assembly lines. For the first time, there was standardization in production, allowing industrial businesses to grow even more. These developments also helped keep production costs down by creating higher efficiency in industrial processes. During this period, automobiles became a technology for everyone, creating a more mobile society. People begin commuting to work for the first time. Mass production also led to a rise in the need for raw materials, causing even more expansion in other industries.

> # Key to the fifth technological wave was the invention of the microprocessor, introduced by Intel in 1971.

The increasing use of oil-based products and the emergence of electronics also marked this wave. Although many household electronics became available during the tail end of this period, computers and electronics also emerged and were developed for military, academic, and corporate environments. Prices continued to fall, women entered the workforce to a greater extent, and multinational corporations were born. The wave came to an end with two major oil crises in the final decade, beginning with organization of the petroleum exporting countries (OPEC) members proclaiming an oil embargo in 1973, resulting in oil shortages, worldwide stock market crashes and a global recession.

INFORMATION AND COMMUNICATION (1970s TO 2010s)

Key to the fifth technological wave was the invention of the microprocessor, introduced by Intel in 1971. This allowed information handling to be installed everywhere, making mass communication possible. During this period, home electronics developed rapidly, with many households having toasters, microwaves, computers,

BROADEN YOUR TECHNOLOGY PERSPECTIVE

MEGATRENDS

TECHNOLOGIES

CASES

FRAMEWORK

EXECUTION

TECHSTORM 44

and multiple television sets. Communication was dramatically changed by the inventions and rise of fax machines, cellular phones, email, and the internet.

As with the technology of the other waves, the effect of the microprocessor was not realized at once. At first, computers were used by only governments and universities. However, the technology continued to develop and become increasingly affordable, mostly due to the exponential development known as Moore's law, where, in simple terms, computer performance doubles approximately every two years. The general population was able to take advantage of this new technology, just as they had with the advances in automobiles during the fourth wave. Using computer technology, small businesses were able to find a way to make more of an impact. While this did not put an end to mega-corporations, it did lead to a vast increase in business networks and cooperation in development.

One of the most interesting developments of the fifth technological wave is that even though there was a massive increase in communication, there was also a continuing increase in transportation. Therefore, a need for more flexible energy solutions became more pressing to make this possible. Society is now on the verge of a sixth technological wave following the 2008 financial crisis.

THE THREE PHASES OF A TECHNOLOGY WAVE

Although the technology surrounding each technology wave seems vastly different, there is a clear development that all technologies must go through to reach widespread adoption[39]: experimentation, expansion, and transformation. One of the most important factors to consider is that the guiding principles for decision making and our relationship to technology will change as frequently as does the technology itself. The principles used today to make decisions regarding how to use technology will not necessarily apply in tomorrow's world.

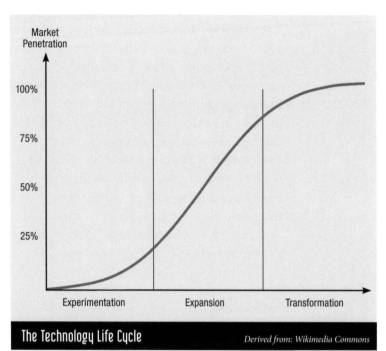

Market
Penetration

100%

75%

50%

25%

Experimentation   Expansion   Transformation

The Technology Life Cycle *Derived from: Wikimedia Commons*

EXPERIMENTATION

During the experimentation phase of the technological wave, an outdated technology starts to be replaced by a new one, but there aren't immediate or major improvements in functionality. For example, the first cars were called "horseless carriages" and very much resembled actual carriages. In the early stages, this was simply a substitution for a means of transportation that already existed. In the experimentation phase, society often instills total trust in the new technology, expecting it to change everything eventually, yet public perception is more curious and questioning than embracing.

The first cars that were introduced were not that impressive or even better than other means of transportation. They were called "horseless carriages" and were more expensive, noisy and polluting than horse drawn carriages. On top of that, they were no faster than a horse and carriage. This initial "exploring" phase for a fresh technology occurs when the technology introduced is not necessarily an improvement, but rather a new way of doing things. Here the rate of experimentation and innovation is high, and the number of application areas can expand rapidly.

EXPANSION

After the experimentation phase, comes the expansion phase. The new technology improves, leading to a significant increase in demand. The technology then spreads to more and more users, and society eventually gets used to it. Again looking at the automobile example, more people began using cars, driving them to work and travelling around the country. During this expansion phase, productivity improves and the technology is adjusted to fit society's needs.

When cars grew faster, more reliable and more affordable, their prevalence increased, changing our behavior. People started using cars to go to meetings or visit relatives who lived some distance away. Trucks were used to transport goods. The technology became more and more accepted.

BROADEN YOUR TECHNOLOGY PERSPECTIVE

MEGATRENDS

TECHNOLOGIES

CASES

FRAMEWORK

EXECUTION

TECHSTORM 44

TRANSFORMATION

In the final phase, called transformation, society is restructured. Not only will more and more people be using the new technology at this stage, but society itself adapts to its use. For example, owning a car became more widespread during this phase and car ownership became a social norm, rather than a luxury. This led to a huge increase in traffic and the development of suburbs, shopping malls and drive-in cinemas, things that could not have existed previously. The new technology merges with a new way of thinking, and the full potential is realized.

The peak of a new technology is when it reaches its full potential, becomes commonly accepted and fundamentally changes our lives and society. With the car, this occurred in the 1940s and 1950s, at least in the Western world. As a natural consequence, we could then see the emergence of suburbs, shopping malls and drive-in cinemas, phenomena that would otherwise have been impossible. Our way of living and working had totally changed because of a new technology.

TECHNOLOGY WAVES AND ECONOMIC PROGRESS

There is a significant correlation between a technology wave and economic progress. The model opposite is based on the notion that capitalist economies have long cycles of boom and bust, fuelled by technology and society's progress during each wave. These cycles are typically 40-60 years long, and as previously stated, each wave goes through three phases related to technological development and acceptance.[40]

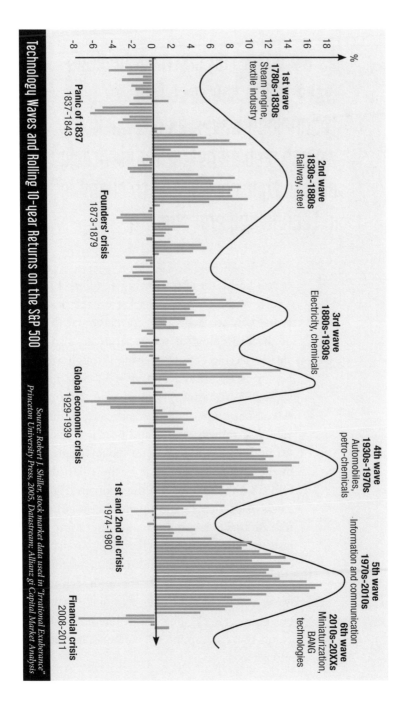

Technology Waves and Rolling 10-year Returns on the S&P 500

1st wave
1780s-1830s
Steam engine,
textile industry

2nd wave
1830s-1880s
Railway, steel

3rd wave
1880s-1930s
Electricity, chemicals

4th wave
1930s-1970s
Automobiles,
petro-chemicals

5th wave
1970s-2010s
Information and communication

6th wave
2010s-20XXs
Miniaturization,
BANG
technologies

Panic of 1837
1837-1843

Founders' crisis
1873-1879

Global economic crisis
1929-1939

1st and 2nd oil crisis
1974-1980

Financial crisis
2008-2011

Source: Robert J. Shiller, stock market data used in "Irrational Exuberance",
Princeton University Press, 2005, Datastream; Allianz gi Capital Market Analysis

As we enter the sixth technology wave, using the first five technology waves as our guide, we can prepare better for inevitable events that correspond to changes in technology and society.

If you build a graph showing a rolling 10-year return of the US stock market for the past 200 years, you see a distinct correlation with four of the technological waves. You can also very clearly see the economy going through a number of crises. The "panic of 1837" was mainly caused by runaway prices of land, cotton and slaves. The crisis of 1873 was because of inflated values of railway shares and post-war financial turmoil. There followed the Great Depression in the 1930s, the oil crisis in the 1970s due to OPEC's oil embargo, and the Lehman triggered stock market crash and financial crisis of 2008. It's safe to say technology waves are more than just repeating patterns. They can, in fact, be used to understand the future of economy and society better. As we enter the sixth technology wave, using the first five technology waves as our guide, we can prepare better for inevitable events that correspond to changes in technology and society.

THE FUTURE OF TECHNOLOGY

MEGATRENDS

TECHNOLOGIES

CASES

FRAMEWORK

EXECUTION

TECHSTORM 44

Precisely what the future has in store for business and society is unclear, but the development of emerging technologies gives a great glimpse into just how the world might develop in the coming decades. As scientific advances in nanotechnology, genomics, and neuroscience continue, the world seems, paradoxically and simultaneously, more complex and simpler.

To get a clearer picture of where this emerging techstorm will take us, it is necessary to try to understand what the next GPT is. As we have seen in the past, it is the GPTs that drive the major technological waves that lead to these vastly different societies that wouldn't even be clearly recognizable to previous generations.

There is little doubt that the next GPT that will lead us into the sixth wave already exists. While this GPT is still in its infancy, it has given way to many emerging technologies that will also shape the different possible courses of the future. The GPT that seems most likely to bring us into a vastly different world is nanoscience,

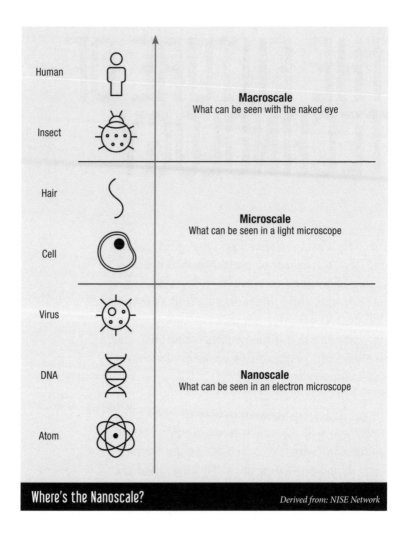

		Macroscale
Human		What can be seen with the naked eye
Insect		

Microscale
What can be seen in a light microscope

Hair

Cell

Virus

Nanoscale
What can be seen in an electron microscope

DNA

Atom

Where's the Nanoscale?   *Derived from: NISE Network*

miniaturization and our ability to understand and interact on molecular and atomic scales.

MINIATURIZATION - THE NEXT BIG THING

Nanoscience is a rapidly growing field that has the potential to create an entirely new generation of scientific and technological approaches.[41]

With nanoscience, there is a completely new understanding of the atomic scale and how it can be used. By focusing on the atom and how it can be manipulated and used, nanoscience opens the doors for many fresh possibilities in IT, materials science, medicine, and life itself. Nanoscience refers to the study of objects that fall in the nanometer scale, which ranges from 1 to 100 nanometers, and includes studies of viruses, DNA and material properties on the atomic scale. The ability to study and understand objects on such a small scale certainly is an impressive feat that will greatly enhance the understanding of the world around us.

While nanoscience may be something that is far beyond the grasp of understanding for the average person today, this developing GPT is something that will put us on the course to a dramatically different understanding in the future. According to the US National Nanotechnology Initiative, "The emerging fields of nanoscience and nano-engineering are leading to an unprecedented understanding and control over the fundamental building blocks of all physical things. These developments are likely to change the way almost everything is designed and made."[42] This new understanding of the way things work will allow for a future in which everything can be made differently.

A COMBINATION OF SCIENCES

Although the term "nanotechnology" was introduced by physicist Richard Feynman in 1959, nanoscience is a relatively new field. Fueled by innovations in imaging and interaction on the atomic scale during the end of the twentieth century, the field has seen tremendous development in the past 15 years and its role as a GPT is already becoming solidified. Nanoscience is also unique in that it combines physics, chemistry, and biology in a way that scientific fields have not generally done before.

WHY SO SMALL?

One of the biggest questions concerning nanoscience is why things need to be broken down to such a small scale. The very idea of nanoscience requires objects to be very small. "Smaller is better" could actually be a principle of nanoscience, at least in certain terms and to a certain extent. Computers are an excellent example of this principle. The massive increase in the speed of computers has not been accompanied by larger devices. In fact, it is the smaller device that allows the computers to be faster. By exploring smaller avenues, we are able to put more and more power into a smaller chip, thus giving us something much faster without having to increase size. Without nanoscience, this shrinking of computers would have been impossible.

By granting the ability to study objects of such small sizes, nanoscience allows for greater understanding and analysis. In turn, this allows for advancements in manufacturing, modification, and many other areas. Nanoscience as a GPT has many applications and has already led,

MEGATRENDS   TECHNOLOGIES   CASES   FRAMEWORK   EXECUTION   TECHSTORM 44

and will, in the coming years, continue to lead to incredible progress in many emerging fields and technologies.

The great advance in computer processing power also makes it possible to study microbiological and neural systems at a much more detailed level, completing the connection between four major branches of science. Combining IT with nano-technology, neuroscience and biotechnology and medicine, is popularly referred to as "BANG technologies": bits, atoms, neurons and genes.

The small scale used in nanoscience has led to significant advances in medicine. By exploring cells at their natural level, scientists are able to create more effective methods of interacting with cells. Instead of using larger instruments to affect the behavior of cells, nanoscience has allowed for the usage of tiny particles, no big-ger than the cells themselves. In doing so, nano-science creates better ways to fight complex health problems such as viruses and cancer. The answer to defeating cancer isn't by attacking it with something bigger; it's a matter of getting down to the right size to explore, analyze, and combat it most effectively.

IS NANOSCIENCE REALLY THE NEXT GPT?

In order to consider nanoscience as a GPT, it must have four basic characteristics. First, nanoscience is a single generic technology. While nanoscience itself can be hard to classify into one definition, it is essentially the study and use of objects on a very small scale. All advances in nanoscience involve looking at these very small building blocks. Therefore, it is a single technology. It is generic in scope in that it can apply to the study of any small particles. Nanoscience does not refer to only a specific study but rather a broad one.

> **Nanoscience is pushing us into a new technological wave that will leave our world unrecognizable to our current minds.**

The second question, whether or not nanoscience has scope for improvement and development, is simple to answer. There are billions of small objects to be explored in a variety of fields, and nanoscience has only scraped the surface so far, although the technology is developing quickly. The advances already have made a significant impact on society and everyday life, but the potential for improvement seems virtually unlimited at this point. Computers can be made faster, fuels more efficient, and bodies stronger and more resistant to viruses and diseases. The key to achieving all this is nanoscience.

The third characteristic of a GPT is that it must be used widely and have multiple uses in its mature state. Nanoscience is still maturing, but its many uses are already apparent. From biology to computer processing, to environmental systems, to manufacturing, nanoscience seems to have the ability to reach nearly every field. As nanoscience continues to mature and develop, more and more uses seem inevitable.

The final characteristic of a GPT is the requirement for spillovers into other areas of society and economy. As seen already, nanoscience has the potential to affect all areas of society. From a potential economic impact of trillions of dollars, to a healthier society that can manufacture its own goods to exact specifications, there seems to be no limit to the reach of nanoscience.

There is virtually no doubt that nanoscience meets all the necessary characteristics to qualify as a GPT. The only question that then remains is whether or not this is the GPT that will lead the next technological wave.

SMALL BUT FAR REACHING - CROSS POLLINATION

As much as nanoscience has already changed our lives, its potential is far from realized. With the possibilities of cures for cancer as well as the prospects of artificial intelligence, new materials with unique properties, and many other things we cannot yet imagine on the horizon, nanoscience is pushing us into a new technological wave that will leave our world unrecognizable to our current minds.

Nanoscience may deal with only the very small, but its impact is going to be very big. Maybe the most fascinating aspect of nanoscience is that it spans many disciplines and creates interesting interactions. The concept of cross-pollination between different disciplines is one of the most exciting aspects of science today. This is also happening between science and the arts, for example the CERN (European Organization for Nuclear Research) particle accelerator creates scholarships for artists-in-residence, physicists use modern dance to find new metaphors for quantum dynamics and (on a more applied level) material scientists are finding inspiration from biological systems – shark skins for low friction wet suits and gecko "toes" for upgraded adhesives.

ENVIRONMENTAL ASPECTS OF NANOSCIENCE

While the emergence of nanoscience has created some concerns about the future of the environment, it also has the potential to provide solutions. Research into nanoparticles and their potential effects on the environment is currently limited, but studies concerning other small particles, including airborne pollutants, suggest the possibility of some major impacts that may also be seen with nanoscience. The main questions regarding nanoparticles and the environment center on how these small particles will behave in existing environmental systems. It is possible that nanoparticles could enter into the food chain and interfere with certain biological processes. In order to use nanoscience to help the environment, it will be essential to understand and address these issues.

The growth and development of nanoscience and nanoparticles points to more good than harm for the environment. However, it appears possible to use nanoparticles to make pollutants into less harmful chemicals. Because of the size and volume of nanoparticles, they take on a reactive nature that can speed up chemical reactions. This has already been put to use in the US, with nanoparticles being explored as a way to remove pollutants from ground water and soil.

There are certainly many unanswered questions about just how nanoscience will impact the environment in the future, but current developments suggest that the benefits will be very positive for the world. By creating more efficient energy sources and doing a better job of eliminating pollutants, this emerging area of technology has great potential to solve some of the biggest problems facing the world today.

MEGATRENDS

TECHNOLOGIES

CASES

FRAMEWORK

EXECUTION

TECHSTORM 44

BANG – THE SIXTH TECHNOLOGY WAVE

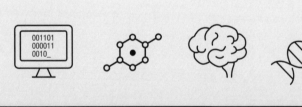

BANG technologies - Bits, Atoms, Neurons, Genes

While most of these emerging technologies are still in relatively early phases of development and growth, we are already starting to understand the potential and implications. The possibilities made achievable by these technologies could not have been imagined 50 years ago. It is impossible to determine exactly how these technologies will look at their peak, but it is certain that they will have a major impact on life, as we know it. Bits, as in information and communication technologies; atoms, as in nanotechnology and innovations in our physical environment; neurons, as in neurotechnology and our understanding of the brain; genes, as in medicine, biotechnology and genetics.

BITS

The rapid expansion of networks and computing systems has already created a world that seems very different to that of even just a few years ago. Computing systems have become more powerful while getting smaller, and one of the most amazing things about computer technology over the years is that a super computer that once took up an entire room can now fit into the palm of your hand, for a fraction of the price.

Two major advances in communication technologies are the fiber optic cable and rapidly increasing mobile broadband. Although these have been around for several years, they continue to improve at a rapid pace, allowing for millions of bits of information to be delivered in fractions of a second. The demand for high speed communication continues to increase, and networks are constantly being developed to meet these demands.

With more than 1.9 billion people using mobile internet on a daily basis, it is clearly more than just a way of browsing for the latest gossip.[43]

People are able to stay connected all the time, allowing for more possibilities no matter where they are. The quality of internet-based services continues to grow, and there is now an application for pretty much everything.

Computing systems are not just becoming faster and smaller. They are also becoming smarter. With a greater ability to track preferences and customize user experiences, computing systems are on the verge of acting like the human brain. While this may sound frightening to some, it also gives us a greater ability to understand the human brain, which has obvious spillovers into neuro-technology.

The concept behind artificial intelligence is certainly nothing new to our society. In fact, artificial intelligence has been a concept since Alan Turing first imagined a computer that "passed" as a human in 1950.[44] Creative minds have long explored, through novels, movies, and other mediums, the possibility of artificial intelligence and what it might mean for the future of the world. While artificial intelligence is not fully conceived in our world today, it is probably on the cusp of reality. From robots that can perform manufacturing tasks to exact specifications, to computers that can diagnose cancer with better accuracy than an average doctor,[45] there is no doubt that computers are becoming smarter.

While there are plenty of examples of computers beating humans in game shows and arcade games, the machine's inability to recognize the subtleties

MEGATRENDS

TECHNOLOGIES

CASES

FRAMEWORK

EXECUTION

TECHSTORM 44

of language that are easily detected by the human mind shows the current limitations. Still, artificial intelligence is growing closer and will likely be a driving force in the next technological wave. Additionally, major corporations such as Google, Microsoft, IBM, and even Facebook are investing huge sums of money in artificial intelligence. From developing larger tracking systems that can think rather than just accumulate data, to creating computer programs capable of recognizing the difference between a fake smile and a genuine one, these industry giants are exploring the many potentials of artificial intelligence technology. In the near future, advanced computational power will initially be a competitive advantage, then swiftly afterwards a pure necessity.

ATOMS

Nanotechnology, arguably the most direct effect of nanoscience, involves the manipulation of matter at the atomic and molecular level. Compared with nanoscience, being the enabler, nanotechnology is more concerned with direct applications. Nanoscience has much broader implications as a GPT. Rather than looking at nanotechnology as a way of miniaturizing things, this emerging technology should be regarded as a way to use smaller pieces in order to create structures that have brand new properties such as strength, flexibility, weight, and so on.

The primary function of nanotechnology involves engineering at a molecular scale, and this allows for multiple methods. The more original approach is described as a "bottom up" method. Here, materials and devices are created from molecular compounds. With the bottom-up approach, smaller components are arranged into more complex constructions or assemblies. An example of bottom-up is seen in DNA nanotechnology, in which well-defined structures are constructed out of DNA and nucleic acids. On the other hand, the "top-down" approach involves nano-objects that are created from larger entities. There is no atomic level control, and the goal is to create smaller devices by utilizing the assembly of something larger. The creation of smaller and smaller microprocessors is one example of the top-down approach.

> Today, nanotechnology exists in a range of available products, including paints, new materials and novel approaches to in situ delivery of targeted medication.

The pioneers of nanotechnology envisioned a world in which anyone could assemble exactly what they wanted. This vision focused on a machine that could allow people to create anything from food to clothes to electronics, atom by atom.[46] Of course, this vision still seems quite far fetched today, but nanotechnology does have many practical implications in society.

MEGATRENDS

TECHNOLOGIES

CASES

FRAMEWORK

EXECUTION

TECHSTORM 44

The commercialization of nanotechnology is still in its infancy, but funding and scientific advance is helping this grow rapidly. Today, nanotechnology exists in a range of available products, including paints, new materials and novel approaches to in situ delivery of targeted medication. Although we can't see it, these products are based on nanoparticles, and these nanoparticles have allowed for advances in many industries. Nanotechnology is also responsible for virtually all computer-based technology, including the quick charging mobile phone batteries that help make our daily communications so convenient. Solar power, fuel cells, computer screens, and many other things we encounter daily also take advantage of nanotechnology.

"Atoms", as part of the BANG metaphor, also includes other technology advances in the physical world, for example 3D printing and the rapidly developing maker movement. The field of robotics is another field that has seen many major advances in the past few years, and there are big things on the horizon. Robots are becoming more and more powerful, with the ability to perform more and more like humans. From factory robots who can now work alongside humans, to robots who can play sports and ride bikes, robotic technology is showing the potential to transform both industry and everyday life.

Robots are also being designed to make jobs easier and safer. A wearable "agrirobot" suit can reduce the amount of energy required to harvest crops out in the fields. Other robots have been able to apprehend criminals and safely search them for explosives. Developments in robotics may also assist in day-to-day movement, from helping elderly people walk up the stairs to reducing the stress on the body required by hours of standing or physical labor.

NEURONS

Neuroscience is also improving because of a greater understanding of how the brain works. Several new major brain mapping initiatives are attempting to simulate or map all neural connections in the human brain, and projects like this will allow researchers to track the activity of individual neurons in real time.[47] Current brain mapping projects have focused on static images of the brain, while the new initiatives aim to record all the activity of millions of neurons. These initiatives will provide a much greater understanding of how the brain works, including a better understanding of language, perception and cognition.

Another major development in neuroscience is the ability to hardwire human thoughts into a machine or robot. An experiment by Honda recently allowed a human to control a robot through brainpower. While wearing a special brain activity helmet, a person was able to dictate a robot's actions using nothing but brainpower. This technology could be used throughout society, giving people the ability to perform tasks just by thinking about them. For example, inventors of this particular technology see humans eventually being able to turn on the air conditioning

BROADEN YOUR TECHNOLOGY PERSPECTIVE

MEGATRENDS

TECHNOLOGIES

CASES

FRAMEWORK

EXECUTION

TECHSTORM 44

or open doors through brainpower. With a better understanding of the human brain, combined with improvements and innovations in precision mechanics, major advancements have been made in the field of prosthetics. Today, the most advanced artificial limbs can be hard-wired into a human brain and controlled directly by the user's thoughts.

Also, today researchers combine a deep understanding of how the brain functions and where actions and thought processes occur, with genetic engineering and fiberoptics. Enter the field of optogenetics, where researchers use light to alter the activity of genetically modified neurons, and through that being able to control a subject's behavior. Pure science-fiction and very dystopic, but also used to restore auditory activity and treating drug abuse.

GENES

Another emerging technology field that has had a great impact on society and will likely have an even more significant one in the future is the combined field of biotechnology and genetics. Together, these fields allow for a much greater use and understanding of living things. In synthetic biotechnology, living systems and organisms are, among other things, used to develop products or processes that have a specific use, be it engineering organisms to produce various kinds of biological products and renewable fuels, or using cells as microscopic molecular foundries to produce genetically encoded materials.[48]

Biotechnology is certainly not a new invention. Humans have arguably used biotechnology for thousands of years, in areas ranging from agriculture to food production and medicine. If we use a broad definition of biotechnology, cultivating plants can be considered the first biotechnological enterprise. While agriculture certainly was a breakthrough that revolutionized lives and affected society, the biotechnology we are exploring today is something much more exciting and transformative. Modern biotechnology has allowed for the development of antibiotics, which have certainly helped to advance and improve society. Still, this is hardly the biotechnology that we know today and will come to know in the near future. Even the modern version of biotechnology has been around for more than 40 years, its roots embedded in the first successful gene splicing experiments of the early 1970s.

Although biotechnology is nothing new, it is on the verge of a breakthrough that will transform society. Within a few years, biotechnology will most probably "enable us to identify, understand, manipulate, improve, and control living organisms (including ourselves)".[49] Today's biotechnology includes some rather sophisticated and impressive fields of science, including genomics and immunology.

Biotechnology's effects will be seen in almost all main areas of industry, including healthcare, agriculture, non-food products such as biofuels, and the environmental sector. Modern biotechnology already has a wide range of uses, including the use

MEGATRENDS

TECHNOLOGIES

CASES

FRAMEWORK

EXECUTION

TECHSTORM 44

of organisms to manufacture organic food products, and the use of natural bacteria in bioleaching for the mining industry. Of course, the reach of biotechnology extends well beyond these areas, also allowing for improvements in recycling, waste treatment and cleanup. In a sense that few would regard as beneficial, biotechnology is also responsible for a threatening, and potentially very harmful, area of biological warfare.

Developments in medicine thanks to nanoscience are starting to allow for earlier disease detection and better treatment. Nanoparticles used in medical instrumentation for example amplify images in order to give a better glimpse of what is at work in the body. The smaller the area that can be explored, the better the chance of diagnosing a disease before it spreads. For some diseases, like Salmonella and other food borne pathogens, rapid detection is essential in order to deliver treatment before patients deteriorate. Colour enhanced scanning and other tools made possible by nanoscience have allowed for quick detection that can save lives.

Regenerative medicine is another advancement that is considered a possible new revolution in healthcare. One of the major areas of research involves stimulating damaged tissue into healing itself. When tissue can regenerate itself, there is no need to introduce foreign substances to the body that may or may not have dramatic side effects. This same process is also leading to the ability to grow tissue and organs that could then be used as implants or compatible prosthetics.

CHARACTERISTICS OF A PARADIGM SHIFT

In times of a maturing GPT, which is the case for IT today, and a rapidly growing successor (nano-science) a number of traits can be identified. What is interesting here is that this has also been true in earlier shifts between GPTs, for example when steam power was succeeded by electricity and the factory system as enabling technologies.

Looking back and analyzing earlier paradigm shifts, a number of interesting patterns emerge as signs of these changing times:

• An unusual expansion in the number of innovations and technological changes. It seems as if one invention leads to another, and that there are local, regional and national effects working together to form a positive environment for innovation and technological change.

BROADEN YOUR TECHNOLOGY PERSPECTIVE

MEGATRENDS

TECHNOLOGIES

CASES

FRAMEWORK

EXECUTION

TECHSTORM 44

- Improvements and innovations in technology are closely followed by improvements in communication as well as physical transportation.
- Production and distribution of power has paved the way for, or closely followed, innovations. In this ongoing shift, we are still waiting for the breakthrough in energy and battery technologies, although interesting prospects are easily identifiable today.
- Disruptive technology innovation will change business development constantly, but there are some more fundamental ongoing principles that are valid today and tomorrow.

Also, there are a number of individual, corporate and social traits that become visible and change in these times of technological paradigm shifts.

NEW PERSPECTIVE ON TIME

Today businesses instinctively choose speed as a business development strategy, using advanced computer software, social networks and mobile communication to stay agile. We have seen that logistics, transportation and communication systems have been vastly developed during most of the five technological waves, and these have been among the main drivers since then. This is also true in manufacturing where most industries boast that parts remain only hours in factories before leaving as components of a finished product. The definition of real time in this context is that an automated system can actually keep up with the job, processing input with no delay to output. Now companies have real time scheduling, analyzing and action in production as well as in other parts of their daily processes. This has expanded in business and will have a great impact on organizations, individual employees and speed of work.

> **The notion that society is moving faster will affect everyone, and sociologists have found that increasing wealth and education bring a sense of tension about time.**

INCREASING SPEED OF TIME

The move to a real time perspective does not only concern business. The notion that society is moving faster will affect everyone, and sociologists have found that increasing wealth and education bring a sense of tension about time. We believe that we possess too little of it. The increasing speed of time is changing the way we behave in business. "In the world before FedEx, when 'it' could not absolutely, positively, be there overnight, it rarely had to. Now that it can, it must. Overnight mail, like so many of the hastening technologies, gave its first business customers a competitive edge. When everyone adopted overnight mail,

BROADEN YOUR TECHNOLOGY PERSPECTIVE

MEGATRENDS

TECHNOLOGIES

CASES

FRAMEWORK

EXECUTION

TECHSTORM 44

equality was restored, and only the universally faster pace remained."[50]

Not only is this acceleration of time affecting us as people, it is also affecting products and services in the marketplace. The lean start-up philosophy is based on the idea that new products and services should reach the market very early and that customer behavior must be closely monitored in order to provide instant feedback and fast product iterations.

CONSTANT LEARNING

"In the knowledge society, the knowledge base is the foundation of the economy", said Peter Drucker, the father of management theory.[51] The focus on ongoing professional development is still valid, and the fast expansion of the knowledge-based workforce is a clear trend. The body of professionals whom Drucker identified as "knowledge workers" 40 years ago, are most in demand, and will remain so. Professional training schools are growing at 100 times the rate of academic institutions, according to KPMG, which estimates that 75% of today's workforce needs retraining. Fortunately, we are entering a new era of educational experience. As a result, there will be more progress in terms of educational content and methodology in the next 10 years than there was in the whole of the past century, ranging from interactive education to networked learning and online university degrees. Also, information systems will push organizational evolution towards decentralization.

Newer, more open organizational models will attract people who are capable of thinking and making decisions for themselves. Even the best men and women need guidance and ongoing learning to enable them to use and analyze new information and to make the best decisions. Companies also need clear strategies for attracting and retaining talented employees.

KNOWLEDGE TRANSFER IN ORGANIZATIONS

In the transformation phase, it is even more essential for corporations to embrace the wisdom that "knowledge is only valuable and helpful when it is being used." Many companies have the best pieces of knowledge and information isolated in individual people or systems such as marketing research, financial data and product development. Corporations need to create policies, systems and cultures that encourage the sharing of this knowledge by improving access systems for employees and also developing better interfaces to capture and find information. Furthermore, it is today increasingly common for a company to involve customers in knowledge creation and analysis, often in the development of new products and services. Of course, there is a risk that this knowledge may find its way to the wrong people; perhaps this risk has to be accepted and weighed against the benefits.

It is of high importance to ensure that knowledge stays in the company even when people leave for new jobs. It is also clear that there is a need for better incentives for knowledge transfer programs. Since the value of modern corporations is tightly linked to their employees' knowledge, an expansion of knowledge transfer and capturing will generate returns in the long term.

Organizations need to pinpoint the knowledge they are lacking and identify the most critical knowledge in order to meet their business goals and to achieve their long term strategies. The next step is to benchmark the quality and speed of transferring knowledge, and to assess how business goals can be linked to existing and future knowledge needs.[52]

MULTI-DISCIPLINARILY ON ALL LEVELS

With new technologies promising customers, managers, and companies the new thing, it is more important than ever for individual employees, as well as the company itself, to have a clear understanding and knowledge of technology from several different angles.

It is therefore important to be up to date on the development of new technologies. This does not necessarily mean that a company has to adopt every new technology, but that it should be aware of its emergence and potential impact.

With this in mind it is as important for everyone to focus on the right technologies as it is to avoid the wrong ones. This is valid not only for companies, but also for individuals and local and regional industry players, as well as governmental institutions. From this, we will see a need for people with multi-disciplinary competences, preferably with a background in business and technology. For people aiming for a future in business, the most important thing might not be being fully educated on every aspect of a technology, but rather understanding the consequences, and being able to see possible applications. The same is also valid on a company level, where corporations need to have a clear understanding of the different competences needed, and then put together teams with diverse backgrounds and expertise.

> For people aiming for a future in business, the most important thing might not be being fully educated on every aspect of a technology, but rather understanding the consequences, and being able to see possible applications.

CROSS-FERTILIZATION OF TECHNOLOGIES

Another trend that is taking us into the future is the increasing convergence and cross-fertilization of technologies. We can see a clear example in the way that the human genome was fully sequenced. Going back to the 1970s, biologists thought this would take centuries, but the original estimate from the Human Genome Project, when initiated in 1990, was for completion in 15 years at a cost of US$3 billion. Through a private initiative headed by Celera Genomics, the invention of automated sequencing machines and vastly increased computing power, the completion date was set for 2005, but was actually achieved in 2001 at a cost of US$300 million.[53, 54] Today, full genome sequencing costs roughly US$1,000 and can be completed in 24 hours.[55]

We now see cross-fertilization between a number of technologies, as described earlier with the BANG analogy. Already we have research groups studying the possibilities of building computers based on strings of DNA. Other scientists are including nanotechnology in their work to develop smaller and faster computers or extremely durable materials. Physicists are teaming up with people from the arts and trying to find new metaphors to explain the complexity of science, and the CERN particle accelerator promotes artists-in-residence programs to gain disparate/different views on their work.

One of the most obvious implications of an interdisciplinary era is that it demands interdisciplinary research. Twenty first century students aiming to become managers will need to know about the interrelationships between biology, physics, philosophy, sociology, and political science, to name a few major disciplines. Universities today remain ill equipped to provide such holistic thinking.

GLOBALIZATION

There has been a globalization peak during the past several hundred years, and companies have evolved from being local to regional, national, multinational, and fully global. We have also seen an enormous increase in mergers and acquisitions activities in the past decades, creating larger and even more global companies. There are more strategic alliances with customers, suppliers and even competitors. The same pattern can be identified among customers strengthening their buying power. This trend is, of course, forced and enabled by the explosion of improved communication technologies, but also by education, freedom, and demographics. Instead of economic imperialism, we see how companies start to practice economic diplomacy, realizing that it is vital to adapt to different cultures. The creation of global marketplaces is also generating highly segmented global bodies of potential customers. We see more and more specialized clusters. No one could have predicted the speed with which Google became a global company. Would it have become market leader if it had only focused on the US market? Globalization is not just a business phenomenon. It is an evolution bringing individuals, organizations, nations and cultures together. Given this significance, every organization is today taking the potential effects of globalization into account when formulating its strategies.

CASE STUDIES

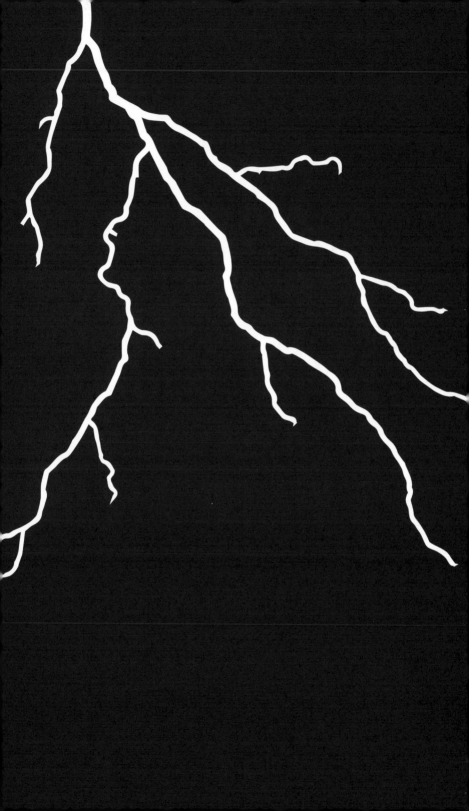

RESCUING THE MUSIC INDUSTRY – SPOTIFY

Right at the peak of the very bullish and bubbly market of 2007, I was affiliated with a large Scandinavian venture capital company. In early spring of that year, an old college friend pitched his new music startup to me. When visiting their office, I remember a couple of things from that first meeting. First, the coffee shop on the ground floor made great espressos. Second, they had a server rack with non-copyrighted music in a closet filled with almost a dozen table fans to remove excess heat. Third, that it was a great idea, and for the next couple of months I was pushing hard to make the investment at an incredibly high valuation for a non-user, non-revenue startup.

The entrepreneurs were definitely on to something, but it was impossible for me to comprehend and convince my colleagues fully that the future of music was streaming access to an almost infinite music catalogue paid for by advertising, not purchasing individual songs or albums and downloading them to your laptop. We passed on the investment, and the company, Spotify, is today one of the most well respected music services with a global reach and a rapidly growing user base. By mid-2015 Spotify had 75 million users, of which 20 million were paying subscribers[56], annual revenues north of US$2.5 billion[57] and a unicorn valuation of more than US$8 billion.[58]

Spotify was founded in late 2006 by Daniel Ek, a young entrepreneur and music geek with a hacker background, and Martin Lorentzon, a highly successful entrepreneur who, the year

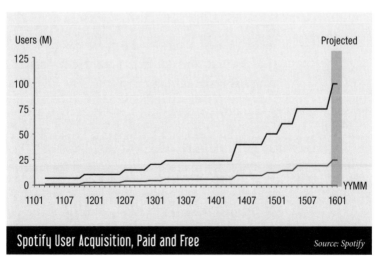

Spotify User Acquisition, Paid and Free   *Source: Spotify*

before, had taken his first start-up public at a US$750 million valuation.

Initially, their idea was nothing more than to make money from advertising. All they needed was to find something to attract a large audience. Soon it dawned on them that the music industry was in really bad shape. Remember that this was in the mid 2000s with an already large, and rapidly growing, music piracy community, a place where all computer-literate music fans hung out. The music industry was in desperate need of a new business model, one that could withstand the coming deadly wave of digitization.

The scope for Spotify was clear from the beginning. Reinvent the music industry with inspiration from hacker culture and music piracy, but with a sustainable revenue model. Also, the goal was to create a streaming music service a lot better than existing peer-to-peer torrent based solutions out there. Speed was of the essence, and Ek and Lorentzon recruited the best programmers available. The first time

The music industry was in desperate need of a new business model, one that could withstand the coming deadly wave of digitization.

MEGATRENDS

TECHNOLOGIES

CASES

FRAMEWORK

EXECUTION

TECHSTORM 44

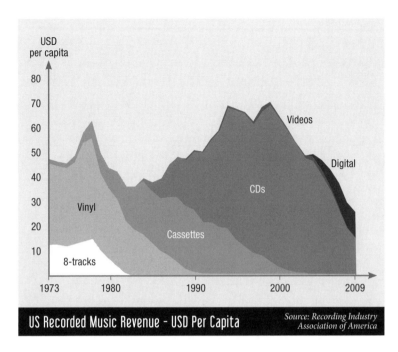

US Recorded Music Revenue - USD Per Capita   *Source: Recording Industry Association of America*

I met the company they were just weeks from releasing the first beta version. The prototype was fast and slick, the concept was intriguing, and it was very clear that they were onto something.

Quite apart from the fact that the founders of Spotify were great visionary entrepreneurs with a total commitment to their cause, they also managed to get the technological timing right. Already in 2006 when Spotify was founded, they saw what was coming:

- a move from downloading to streaming
- the move from desktop to laptop to mobile
- algorithms to analyze and deliver better music recommendations
- cloud based storage of each individual music catalogue

Subscription is at the core of Spotify's business model. Initially, the focus was only on advertising revenues, but after tough negotiations and great pressure from music labels, a paid premium version was introduced.

With giants like Apple and Google having entered the market in recent years, competition is fierce nowadays. Spotify has a large war chest (albeit smaller than its competition), and has forever changed the way we listen to, and pay for, music. Still, only time will tell whether the market position is sustainable in the long run.

THE TABLOID WAR – EXPRESSEN

When the Second World War was nearing its end in late 1944, Swedish tabloid *Expressen* was founded as a reaction to the fascist and Nazi movement in Europe at that time.

For the first 30 years, the newspaper showed steady and impressive growth, reaching a circulation of 600,000 daily copies. Then the early 1970s arrived, and with that, the oil crisis and a global recession. The growth stopped and circulation stabilized at a still impressive 550,000 daily copies.

In 1995 the internet arrived, and with it, the advent of "the new economy" and a time of high expectation and radical change, bigger than in the previous 50 years in total. The paper's circulation plummeted to around 300,000 copies daily. Then in the late 1990s, circulation increased again, by 20% in just a couple of years. At this time, the *Expressen* leadership made a huge and very costly mistake: it cut back on IT spending.

Considering this graph from a year 2000 perspective, it appeared that the internet was just a fad, so maybe the decision was not such a poor one at that specific moment in time. But with hindsight, it is very clear that it was, and the disruption over the past 15 years has been enormous. Today, *Expressen* has a daily circulation of approximately 170,000 copies, and few would bet on there being a paper edition 10, perhaps even five, years from now.

Expressen is a modern incarnation of a classic tabloid, with a fast and often sensational style of reporting, but as a technology transformation case study, it is one of the most impressive I have seen in recent years. In an effort to catch up with its main competitor, *Expressen* has moved development in-house and gone from five to 55 developers in less than two years. In 2015, it is expanding its TV division from 10 to 60 people in six months.

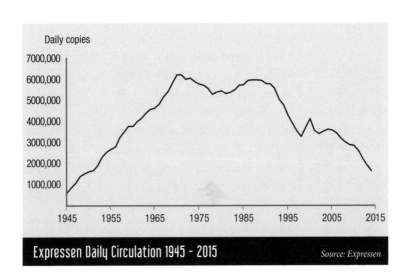

Expressen Daily Circulation 1945 - 2015   *Source: Expressen*

MEGATRENDS

TECHNOLOGIES

CASES

FRAMEWORK

EXECUTION

TECHSTORM 44

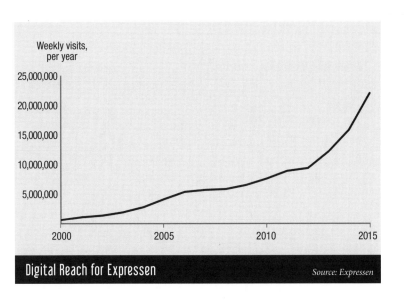

Weekly visits, per year

Digital Reach for Expressen

Source: Expressen

From a strategic perspective, *Expressen* takes a business approach to the fast changing technological landscape. Ten years ago, its readers abandoned the paper edition for desktop computers, and five years ago they left that platform for mobile devices and an app ecosystem. Today, it is all up to the creative and technical abilities of the newspaper to stay ahead of the competition and create new ways of delivering content.

Expressen has a number of priorities that sets it apart from many other media outlets today:

The Swedish media market is relatively small, and therefore all media outlets compete head to head for the same reader audience. In larger markets, media outlets as well as consumers, can afford to be more selective and "niche".

Until recently, *Expressen* used off-the-shelf solutions for online publishing, meaning that it had the same solution as most other players in its marketplace. Today, it has expanded from five to 55 developers who work on unique solutions across all platforms. This means that *Expressen* is now "unique" both in terms of content and in the technology/user experience it offers readers. Compare this to the large, traditional media companies in Europe and the US that use off-the-shelf solutions.

One challenge is that *Expressen*, today, competes directly with media channels in other countries, often venture capital funded and very technology savvy. For example, *Huffington Post* is very well versed in the Google search engine algorithms and can adjust accordingly. Buzzfeed, on the other hand, has expert knowledge of the Facebook technology and ecosystem. To fight this, *Expressen* partners with global media outlets with similar approaches and user bases.

The competitive media landscape is growing ever more complex as publishers venture into new areas. Print media is turning to the web and TV formats, while broadcast media turns to the web and also sometimes to print. To compete with this, *Expressen* launches new niche magazines and follows this up with specific web publications as well as TV channels with news and unique content produced in-house.

COMPUTATIONAL POWER – WOLFRAM RESEARCH

Stephen Wolfram is a living legend, a one-of-a-kind genius who dropped out of Eton and enrolled at Oxford University at the age of 17. Very soon, he found the lectures boring and tedious and left after less than a year. He moved to California, completed college and earned himself a PhD from Caltech before the age of 20. Way to go!

After only a couple of years pursuing an academic career, he founded Wolfram Research in 1987, at the age of 28, with the aim of developing a computational research engine. That is exactly what he did, and today his company has a global reach and employs 700 people working with computational software, programming languages and machine learning. Wolfram Research has been profitable for the past 27 years, so profitable that Wolfram himself took 200 of his colleagues on a 10 year "thinking sabbatical" in the 1990s to work in basic physics research, resulting in a 1,100 page self-published book about computer modeling entitled *A New Kind of Science*.

The main product lines from Wolfram|Alpha today are still Mathematica, the symbolic mathematical computation program, but also the web based Wolfram Alpha computational knowledge engine and Wolfram Language, a general multi-paradigm programming language.

Due to innovations and new applications, business model development can be both an opportunity, and sometimes a necessity, for taking on the competition. Wolfram Research is very interesting because it has a slightly different approach, where in it launches new products and services and then waits for the market to catch up and understand their value. With a sound underlying business, the company can afford to be patient. But, another issue for software companies is that the business models are shifting to freemium and subscription based software as a service offerings as well as app-based models for revenue generation.

Wolfram Research has a 100% focus on technology and application development, give or take. The company is driven by curiosity, and hardly ever consults market research in order to understand what customers want, at least not before a product is launched.

Stephen Wolfram takes pride in NOT following the lean startup model of build – measure – learn, and instead lets his staff explore and innovate without immediate need for market interaction in the development process. When taking on a new project, the timescale is usually at least five years, and sometimes up to 10 years before the result is presented to the market.

The first release of a new product is always very important, not something you throw out to the public, allowing users be judge and jury.

Wolfram Research has been consistently profitable for many years and obviously has a sustainable business model. The company does not consider itself innovative when it comes to business. Instead it can focus its resources on continuous product improvement and creative development of new products.

Regarding technological timing, Wolfram Research is privately held and can afford the luxury to have a very long term approach, both from a technological as well as from a market perspective.

FURNISHING THE WORLD - IKEA

IKEA is one of the largest furniture companies in the world, and through 373 stores in 47 countries, the group will reach a turnover of 30 billion EUR in 2015 and is aiming for 50 billion EUR in 2020. The company was founded in 1943 by Ingvar Kamprad and is still privately owned through an intricate foundation structure with the aim of preserving the business for generations to come.

Ingvar Kamprad, founder said: "I decided early that the stock market was not an option for IKEA. I knew that only a long term perspective could secure our growth plans and I didn't want IKEA to be dependent on financial institutions."

Like all Swedes, and many other people around the world, I have a long lasting relationship with IKEA. Also, our family business was, for a long time, a supplier to IKEA, and we were home to the IKEA office in Romania for almost 10 years in the late 1980s and early 1990s. This means I have followed the development of the company, both through close contact with its operations, and as a customer, sometimes struggling with the assembly of purchased furniture.

From a strategic perspective, IKEA is interesting and impressive in many ways. Still privately owned after more than 70 years in business, still inspired by the thrifty values of its founder, Ingvar Kamprad, and still showing a total dedication to bringing affordable furniture and home decoration to the masses.

IKEA is not risk averse, actually thriving in an environment of risk, uncertainty and ambiguity. Being comfortable with uncertainty and ambiguity is a very valuable competitive advantage. Here is a classic comment from Ingvar Kamprad when an employee argued that a specific project involved a high level of risk:

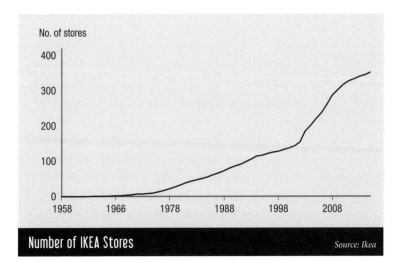

Number of IKEA Stores   *Source: Ikea*

"Yes, I understand, but imagine the possibilities."

IKEA's perspective on time, timing and uncertainty is also very interesting. With a cash reserve of US$15 billion, it can afford to take the long perspective in terms of its investments. Imagine IKEA's entrance into the Russian market in the 1990s, when the economy was in a downward spiral and the political risk was enormous.

> **IKEA is not risk averse, actually thriving in an environment of risk, uncertainty and ambiguity. Being comfortable with uncertainty and ambiguity is a very valuable competitive advantage.**

According to chairman Lars-Johan Jarnheimer, it is relatively simple to enter a new country, and two perspectives are crucial to consider:

1) What long-term potential do we see in the country? Russia, for example, will be a very good market with a large growing middle class population. Here, IKEA also sees it as its mission to offer good quality, affordable furniture to people that need it.

MEGATRENDS

TECHNOLOGIES

CASES

FRAMEWORK

EXECUTION

TECHSTORM 44

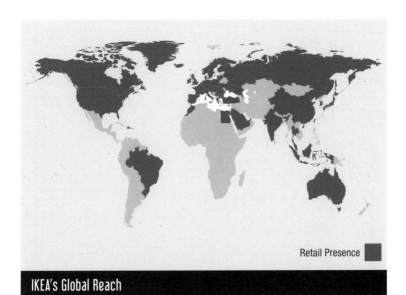

Retail Presence

IKEA's Global Reach

2) How do you provide large-scale economics in your infrastructure, both in the country as well as in a global company perspective?

It is interesting that IKEA often enters a new country through production facilities, meaning that it can grow to understand a local market and culture before establishing stores.

When it comes to technology, IKEA is a rare example of being at the technological forefront, while at the same time working hard to simplify the customer experience and avoiding displaying all the advanced processes that are needed to make it work.

IKEA is pioneering environmental technologies, not (only) as a marketing ploy, but mainly to create a sustainable business and lead where others can follow. With solar panels on the roofs of all its stores, the company will soon be selling energy back to the grid, and the company is also rolling out charging stations for electric vehicles in its car parks all over the world.

Despite all the advanced technology behind the scenes, the company seldom develops its own systems or innovations. At the same time the company has no plans to change its business model other than the obvious and inevitable move from mail order to e-commerce.

From a global perspective, IKEA is shaping the furniture industry, but its adjustments to local market conditions and customer behavior is more like an adopting strategy. That said, it is a fine balance, because too much local adjustment will harm the IKEA brand as well as the global cost leadership through its vast procurement organization.

CREATE
A NEW
FRAMEWORK

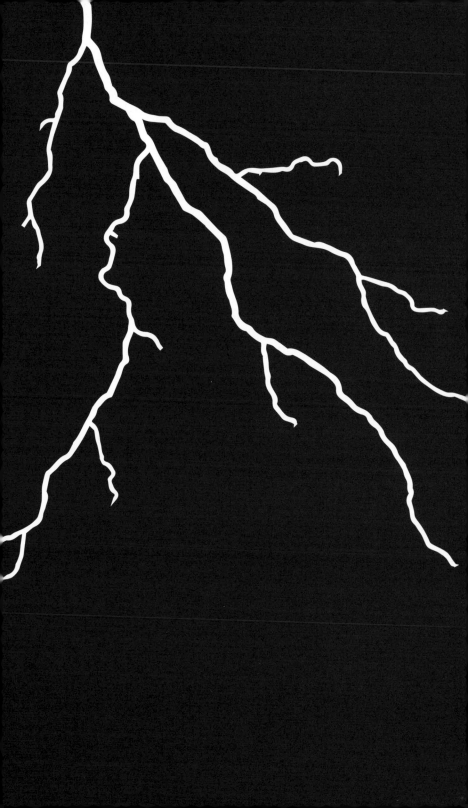

Emerging technologies can be seen as both opportunities and/or threats, depending upon your existing position, viewpoint and mindset. For a startup, a new technology can be its entire reason for being, but there is still an absolute need to understand what is happening in the field. For established companies, or incumbents, emerging technologies are often seen as complicated, time consuming, risky and quite frightening. The reaction to this new reality is often the same.[59] Firstly there is a defensive response where the incumbent believes that the new technology poses a threat to its core business, and secondly a sense of possibilities when the technology shows promise and is too tempting to ignore.

What we see here is situations in which technology and business development intersect and create an interesting, and sometimes highly complex, environment.

History is full of incumbents that have failed to make the transition to new technologies. In 1976, Kodak had a 90% market share of photographic film and 85% of camera sales in the US. The same year, Kodak developed the first digital camera prototype. But because of its fear of cannibalization, destroying its own core purpose, the company lost the battle of film versus digital photography, and as a consequence, went on to lose the camera war by being late into the digital camera market place. Kodak filed for Chapter 11 bankruptcy protection in January 2012, and in early 2013, its digital imaging patent portfolio was acquired by a consortium of 12 licensees including Apple, Google, Microsoft and Samsung.[60]

Another example is Nokia, which overtook Ericsson in the cell phone arena in the late 1990s, when phones went from being B2B products to consumer products. Then in 2007, Nokia was, in turn, overtaken by Apple (and then later by Samsung and Google), when the company failed to catch the wave of large screen smartphones without keyboards.

What we see here is situations in which technology and business development intersect and create an interesting, and sometimes highly complex, environment. Not only do companies have to cope with a new reality of the increasing speed of technological development, they also have to face the challenge of designing new business models that can better cater to the ever-changing needs of customers.

So, from a technology perspective, what pitfalls should an incumbent try to avoid staying competitive in the long run? [61]

One such pitfall is delayed participation, where the incumbent goes for a "wait and see" strategy. This often includes an assignment to an internal

> When choosing to invest in a new technology, one of the biggest challenges to overcome is fear of entering unknown territory.

group or consultants to perform an analysis of potential implications. After that, not much will happen, unless there is a high level executive responsible for continuous monitoring. The reason for delayed participation is often an unwillingness to adapt in anything other than minor incremental innovations. Also, there may be a belief that emerging technologies and innovations will only make negative, or a small positive, impact on the bottom line. Finally, the first products or services based on emerging technologies are often crude and simple, and do not compare well with established offerings.

Another pitfall is sticking with the familiar. When choosing to invest in a new technology, one of the biggest challenges to overcome is fear of entering unknown territory. This can manifest as anything from questioning whether technological shortcomings can be overcome to the choice of future industry standards. From a psychological perspective, aversion to risk and change are two strong human traits. With this in mind, the selling of ideas is always a challenge for those who want to pursue something new.

A further danger is reluctance to commit fully. Incumbents that embrace emerging technologies often do so half heartedly, and there are a number of reasons for that. First, there is the fear of cannibalization of existing products and/ or resistance from the sales force. Second, there exists the managerial paradox "that managers tend toward bold forecasts on the one hand and toward timid choices on the other."[62] Third, when you pitch an innovation against existing business units, the former can rarely compete, from a return on investment perspective; at least not in the beginning. Fourth, managers today are fully focused on their existing businesses and the needs of their current customers. Unless a new technology is demanded by a client, it is hard to get a manager's attention. Finally, it is always a problem for an organization to work with long-term strategy and short term tactics at the same time. The ability to serve existing customer needs while simultaneously exploring potential innovations is extremely challenging.

There may also be lack of persistence, where many incumbents tend to have very little patience when projections are not met and results are not delivered according to plan. This can result from slow market response, aggressive competition in this small market, or the technology itself changing in a fundamental way. A paradox here is that if the core business is faced with challenges, it is very easy to cut its funding. It is also often the case that the people interested in, and responsible for, new technologies and innovations are not represented in the C-suite, and therefore are not sufficiently influential when it comes to company-wide strategic decisions.

So, what could a company do to improve the odds when working with emerging technologies? "Emerging technologies signal their arrival long before they bloom into fully fledged commercial successes. However, the signal to noise ratio is initially low so one has to work hard to appreciate the early indicators. This means looking past the disappointing results, limited functionality, and modest initial applications to anticipate the possibilities. Many signals are available to those who look: other signals can only be seen by the prepared mind. As the philosopher Immanuel Kant noted, we can only see what we are prepared to see. The winners are those who hear the weak signals and can anticipate and imagine future possibilities faster than the competition… The weak signals to be captured usually come from the periphery, where new competitors are making inroads, unfamiliar customers are participating in early applications, and unfamiliar technology or business paradigms are used. However, the periphery is very noisy, with many possible emerging technologies that might be relevant…"[63]

With this comes a learning challenge for the whole organization. The information collected has to be processed, understood and put to good use. Therefore, the incumbent has to foster a culture that is open to different viewpoints, able to challenge existing beliefs and willing to reward experimentation.

When reinventing your business model, there are many similarities with technology innovation. The same obstacles exist: delayed participation; sticking with the familiar; reluctance to commit fully; and lack of persistence. That said, although business model innovation is really difficult, it has changed entire industries. Discount retailers such as Walmart, low cost airlines like Air Asia and Southwest Airlines, software as a service (SaaS) and in-app purchasing have changed entire industries and are good examples of what is possible.

From a strategic perspective, business model innovation is often required when companies are facing any of the following new realities:[64]

- when a large group of potential customers views the existing offering as either too expensive or too complicated
- when it is possible to capitalize on a technology by using a new business model and/ or introducing an established technology to a brand new market segment
- when there is an opportunity to introduce a solution based, rather than a product based, offering to a customer segment
- when there is a need to fight off low end and/or low cost competitors
- when the fundamental basis of competition is changing, often when important market segments are facing commoditization

EXISTING STRATEGY AND LEARNING MODELS

When trying to understand the concept of a business strategy, it is interesting to note that using the terms "business" and "strategy" in the same sentence was unheard of until the 1960s. Before that, "strategy" was a military expression used only to discuss battle tactics.

The word "strategy" is constructed from two Greek words – stratos (army) and ago (to lead). Put together, "strategy" translates into "army leader", and was introduced in ancient Greece in the fifth century BC, where ten strategoi were elected each year to handle both the day-to-day management of building and keeping an army, as well as military or naval expeditions.

Also, in the fifth century BC, Sun Tzu wrote The Art of War. This was the first text on the principles of strategy, and was popularized in the movie *Wall Street* in the 1980s, starring Michael Douglas as Gordon Gekko: "I don't throw darts at a board. I bet on sure things. Read Sun Tzu, *The Art of War*. Every battle is won before it is ever fought."

In modern times, there are a number of well-known management thought leaders who have paved the way for the current approach to business strategy. A few of the key names are Henry Ford and his modern ideas on manufacturing[65, 66], Alfred P Sloan and his thinking on organization and accounting principles[67], Masaaki Imai, who popularized the Kaizen method for continuous improvement[68], and last but not least, the marketing, customer and competitive strategy thinking developed by Peter Drucker[69], Philip Kotler[70], Michael Porter[71, 72] and many more.

OODA

In military terms, strategy and strategic planning take the form of the OODA model, short for observe, orient, decide and act. The concept was originally developed in the US Air Force by Colonel John Boyd[73] and widely used at strategic level. In recent years, the OODA model, or OODA loop, has seen more widespread use in business environment. The major reason for this is the focus on agility and speed, crucial in today's volatile and uncertain market conditions.

MEGATRENDS TECHNOLOGIES CASES **FRAMEWORK** EXECUTION TECHSTORM 44

The OODA loop consists of four very distinct parts that together form a framework for strategic decision making:

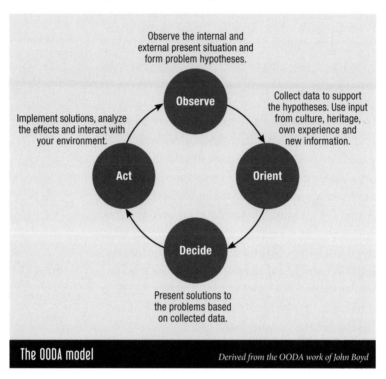

Observe the internal and external present situation and form problem hypotheses.

Observe

Collect data to support the hypotheses. Use input from culture, heritage, own experience and new information.

Implement solutions, analyze the effects and interact with your environment.

Act

Orient

Decide

Present solutions to the problems based on collected data.

The OODA model   *Derived from the OODA work of John Boyd*

LEAN STARTUP

The lean startup methodology is based on the collected experiences of Eric Ries, as a start-up advisor, employee and founder. What started out as a series of blog posts quickly turned into a movement when "the lean startup" was published in September 2011. One of the major underlying themes of the lean startup methodology is the aim of reducing or eliminating uncertainty in business and product development.

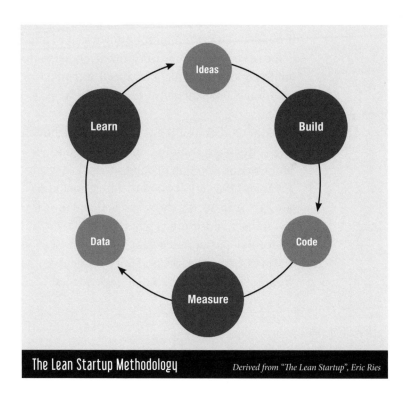

The Lean Startup Methodology   *Derived from "The Lean Startup", Eric Ries*

Some startups abandon all process. According to Ries, they take a "just do it'" approach that avoids all forms of management. But he points out that this is not the only option: "Using the lean startup approach, companies can create order, not chaos, by providing tools to test a vision continuously. Lean isn't simply about spending less money. Lean isn't just about failing fast, failing cheap. It is about putting a process, a methodology around the development of a product."[74]

The basic principle for the lean startup methodology is the process of building something, measuring the response and effect, and then learning from that. This is commonly known as the "build – measure – learn" loop. Also fundamental to the methodology is the focus on speed and on trying to minimize the total time through the loop.

Besides OODA and the lean startup methodologies, there are a number of other ways to view and work on decision making, strategic development and learning. Two of the most well known are PDCA (plan, do, check and act) and the ideas around action learning created by professor and education pioneer Reginald Revans, based on the perspective that the best improvements come from reflection and sharing of experiences.[75]

THE ANALYZE – ASSESS – ADAPT MODEL

Based on my experience and background as an entrepreneur and early stage investor, I realized that all major strategic decisions, whether a strategic move in one of my existing companies or an investment decision in a new venture, are based on a number of factors. These are, first, an understanding of well known megatrends (in this case technology); second, the notion that these trends will change the way a company or industry works; and third, the company's ability to adapt to this volatility, uncertainty and complexity.

With a basic understanding of OODA, action learning and the lean startup models, it is possible to adjust and apply them to the strategic impact of technologies. When trying to understand what is happening in the field of new technologies, it is absolutely necessary to adopt a number of different perspectives before you reach a conclusion.

For this, it is valuable to follow a process that starts with a collection and analysis of information and then turns to an assessment of business implications, before finally arriving at a plan on how to adapt in this new uncertain environment.

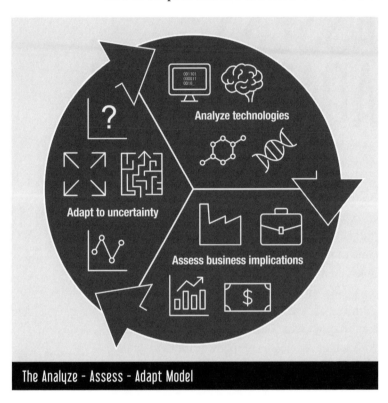

The Analyze - Assess - Adapt Model

The following chapters will present a step-by-step approach to the techstorm, with the goal of identifying and acting on challenges, but most of all opportunities, arising from emerging technologies in an environment filled with uncertainty.

ANALYZE TECHNOLOGIES

A fundamental point about decision-making is that it is done best when it is based on structured information. That said, important business decisions often need to be made in situations where information is scarce and that which is at hand is filled with uncertainty and ambiguity; more on that in the "adapt" section.

Anyway, let us start with the first part of the Analyze – Assess – Adapt process: technology information data gathering and analysis. With today's constant flow of information, it is of course difficult to set aside time to inform yourself of the potential "next big thing" when you have more pressing matters to deal with in running your daily business. But staying on top of current and future technology trends does not have to be complicated nor time consuming. The challenge is to create a new mindset for how to relate to the constant flow of information. Do not for a second believe that it is possible to cover everything; instead be content with the fact that something is a lot better than nothing, and make it a part of your daily routine to follow a number of technology news sources. Scan articles, do not read everything from start to finish or cover to cover. For this exercise, it is often enough to aim for a good overview, before going deeper into a few specific areas. Use fresh perspectives, start using sources that are not necessarily aligned with your world view, ignore trigger warnings and try to move outside of your comfort zone. For example, if you are in favor of genetically modified foods, find a news source that takes a more skeptical view of the area.

So, where do I find this information? Much depends on your interest in technology and your other daily sources of information. The process should be ongoing rather than extremely thorough. Therefore, turning it into a natural part of your daily media consumption is probably the best way to go. That said, it is, of course, important to extend your search beyond your normal routine, meaning going beyond major news channels and industry press to find the stuff that your competitors do not see.

Use fresh perspectives, start using sources that are not necessarily aligned with your world view, ignore trigger warnings and try to move outside of your comfort zone.

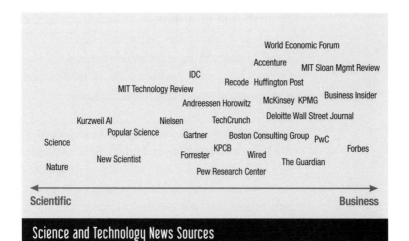

World Economic Forum
Accenture   MIT Sloan Mgmt Review
IDC
Recode Huffington Post
MIT Technology Review
Business Insider
Andreessen Horowitz   McKinsey KPMG
Kurzweil AI   Nielsen   TechCrunch   Deloitte Wall Street Journal
Popular Science   Gartner   Boston Consulting Group   PwC
Science
Forbes
New Scientist   Forrester   KPCB   Wired
Nature   The Guardian
Pew Research Center

Scientific   Business

Science and Technology News Sources

With all this information piling up, be sure to get help from useful software such as RSS feeds and readers as well as social networks; Twitter and LinkedIn are two of the most helpful. Here, it is usually sensible to limit the daily feeds to a few entry points, for example, one RSS-reader and a social network of your choice. Try to avoid overlap, meaning do not subscribe to a RSS-feed and follow the same source on Twitter. Generally it is often a worthwhile following news media through an RSS-reader and individual writers through Twitter or another social media channel.

Finally, be careful to save everything that is even remotely interesting and potentially useful to a device agnostic, online service with good search capabilities. (There is naturally an app for that.)

INFORMATION SORTING

Once an information gathering system is in place, it is time to start making sense of this inflow. There are a number of ways to structure this information about new technologies.

The first thing is to put together a simple list of the 10 most interesting and relevant technologies that will affect the future of your organization. Do not think too much at this stage, just gather information and get it down on paper.

> **Which ones do you believe are the most urgent for your industry? Which ones do you believe will change the playing field the most?**

After you have done this and compiled a list of the most interesting emerging technologies, take some time and try to prioritize among them. Which ones do you believe are the most urgent for your industry? Which ones do you believe will change the playing field the most? Which ones will create new customer demand, and which ones will be the most transformative from an internal process perspective?

For this stage, you could hire expensive consultants, but that takes away one of the main reasons for doing this – you becoming acquainted with

	2015	2020	2025	2030
...				
...				
...				
...				
...				
...				
...				
...				
...				
...				

Ten Most Interesting Technologies

technological progress and where these technologies are taking us. It will help you make better strategic decisions in and about the future of your company or organization, limit the negative impact and reap the benefits of staying ahead of the competition.

When you have gathered interesting, important and essential information on a technology that could be an opportunity and/or a threat, it is time to be a bit more specific about each of your top 10 technologies. To be able to use this information as a strategic tool, it is necessary to try to set two timeframes: for when the technology has passed the peak of hype and survived the walk through the desert; and when a technology has entered the growth phase (we will soon describe these phases). To get some help in this process it is valuable to use a couple of existing models for technology adoption and transformation.

S-CURVE

The three phases of a technology wave introduced earlier is a good starting point. Thinking in terms of experimentation, expansion and transformation makes it quite simple, at least in hindsight, to see how far a technology has come. One interesting thing about using the S-curve is also that it can be seen as a market penetration yardstick where 100% equals the total available market (TAM).

So, the first step is to try to place the emerging technology on the S-curve, most easily done using the experiment, expand, transform analogy. Do not overdo it at the start, the reason for this first exercise is to get everything down on paper and into the graph, not to be totally right. Although, if you want to delve into the S-curve some more, follow the more thorough approach.

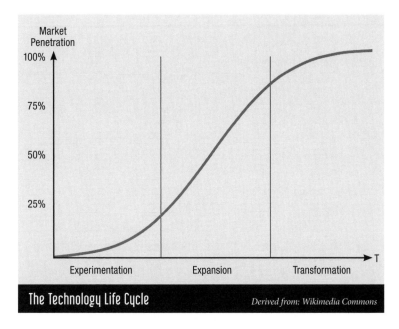

The Technology Life Cycle   *Derived from: Wikimedia Commons*

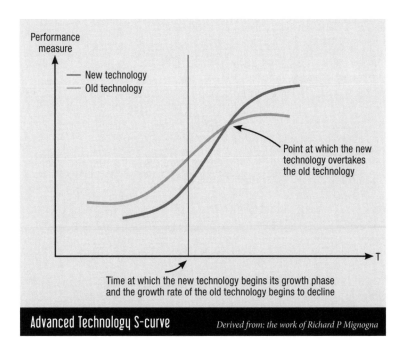

Advanced Technology S-curve   *Derived from: the work of Richard P Mignogna*

In-depth S-curve analysis:[76]
When using the S-curve as a tool for technology analysis, the goal is not to provide precise predictions or present exact conclusions. The focus should instead be on the exploration and learning experience. An extended S-curve technology analysis should include the following steps:

First, you need a defined set of parameters that can describe the advance of the technology as simply as possible. Examples of this can be the storage capacity of solid-state drives (SSDs) or memory cards, the data transmission speed of a cellular network or the cost of sequencing a DNA base pair.

Second, gather data on these specific parameters, but be sure not to complicate matters by mixing different technological measures. For example, do not include hard drives in your data on SSD development or Wi-Fi speed when researching a cellular network capacity.

Third, you have to have a decent understanding of where the technology you are researching is on the S-curve. Since there are always some practical and physical limitations to the performance of all technologies, you have to understand whether the technology itself is on its way to becoming obsolete. If this is the case, you will urgently need to see which technology (or combination of technologies) will be the new standard.

Finally, if a technology substitution seems imminent, do remember that most technology transformations often take longer than initially expected. Also, when an emerging technology is introduced, this usually sparks innovation in areas covered by existing technologies.

HYPE CYCLE

After this initial step applying S-curves to identify technologies, many of those on the top 10 list are often found in a cluster at the beginning of the curve. To be able to distinguish between several technologies in early phases, one needs to use additional tools.

The hype cycle methodology demonstrates how a new technology evolves over time, and can show whether or not it is a viable solution or nothing more than hype.[77] The hype cycle has five main phases that can be used to evaluate a technology. The cycle begins with the *technology trigger*, where a potential technological breakthrough leads to significant interest. In this phase, there is little evidence of commercial

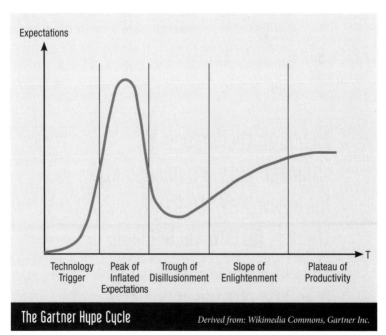

The Gartner Hype Cycle   *Derived from: Wikimedia Commons, Gartner Inc.*

viability, but the technology still incites excitement. The next phase is the *peak of inflated expectations*, where many success stories start to develop, along with plenty of stories of failure as well.

This leads to a third phase, called the *trough of disillusionment*, in which interest begins to wane in light of many failed experiments with the technology. There may still be some investments if there is continued evidence of improvement. The *slope of enlightenment* comes next, in which there are more examples of how the technology might benefit business or society. This leads to new expansions of the technology, but some still remain cautious. Finally, a fifth phase called the *plateau of productivity* occurs, and the technology becomes mainstream. Now it has obvious market viability and the investments start to pay off. It should be no surprise that the GPTs of the technological waves stand up well to the hype cycles. As a result, GPTs

Although technological improvements are necessary for a new wave to exist, there is no new technology that immediately results in a dramatic change in society.

lead to major change in industry, often trans-forming the way manufacturing or distribution is conducted.

TECHNOLOGY ADOPTION CURVE

Although technological improvements are nec-essary for a new wave to exist, there is no new technology that immediately results in a dra-matic change in society. Each new technology that comes into play must go through several phases in order for it to be fully realized to the point that it can have an impact on society and an effect on the future of business. It also must overcome major obstacles on its way to develop-ment, integration and wider market acceptance.

One of the most widespread models is the tech-nology adoption curve[78], stating that a technol-ogy encounters five categories of customers in its lifetime: innovators, early adopters, early majority, late majority, and laggards. The model also introduces a "chasm" that exists between the early adopters (enthusiasts and visionaries) of a technology and the early majority (pragma-tists). The reasoning behind this is that there is a major difference between the expectations of the visionaries and the pragmatists. The tech-nology must successfully transition in the early stages in order to survive and become effective.

The existence of this chasm can prevent tech-nologies from having a major impact on busi-ness and society. A technology cannot cross the chasm without having a target market, a whole

MEGATRENDS   TECHNOLOGIES   CASES   **FRAMEWORK**   EXECUTION   TECHSTORM 44 product concept, a marketing strategy, and other factors that will allow the technology to develop to the point where it can make a significant impact. All these factors pose big challenges to any organization faced with taking the leap from the first initial sales to a more established market presence, and there are numerous examples of technologies that never get past this point. Unless there are enough people on board to see a technology develop, that technology will flounder rather than flourish. Once a technology successfully crosses the chasm, it can begin to have a major impact.

> **Unless there are enough people on board to see a technology develop, that technology will flounder rather than flourish. Once a technology successfully crosses the chasm, it can begin to have a major impact.**

TIMING IS OF THE ESSENCE

You have now identified relevant technologies and have a framework in place to help you estimate their respected approach velocity. Timing is often extremely difficult, but nonetheless of

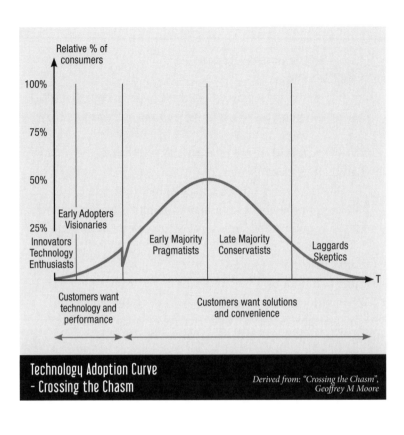

Technology Adoption Curve - Crossing the Chasm

Derived from: "Crossing the Chasm", Geoffrey M Moore

high importance. To be able to take the next step, assessing present and future business implications of emerging technologies, three adoption level milestones are useful to consider: **First**, when the technology makes it onto the radar the first time, early on the hype curve. At this point it is possible to create a brief initial strategic business assessment, which tries to understand the implications of this new uncertainty. **Second**, when the technology has passed the hype and is on its way to reach an early commercial audience. This is the time to keep your eyes open for signs of upcoming mainstream

(Early) initiate project and launch:
(Late) be curious:
Positive media attention and extensive hypeish coverage. Also
look out for conferences with vague focus on the technology.

(Early) sit tight, improve offering and positioning:
(Late) start preparing:
The start of negative media and customer testimonials
pointing at problems and disappointments. Also look out for
startup lay-offs or incumbents closing projects in the field.

(Early) take market shares:
(Late) take action:
When reports are coming out showing positive adaption,
actual (sizable) revenues and package offerings including
products, services and peripherals.

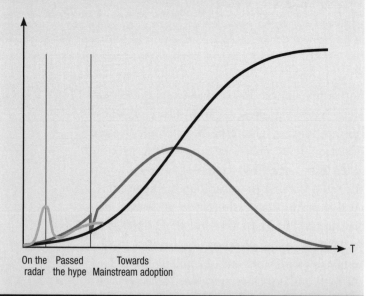

On the   Passed   Towards
radar   the hype   Mainstream adoption

Signs of Adoption - Technology Curves Combined

adoption. **Third**, when the technology has "crossed the chasm" and reached mainstream adoption. Now (at the latest) it is time to launch a full scale effort to handle this new technological landscape.

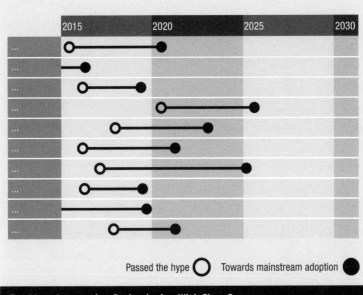

Ten Most Interesting Technologies With Time Frames

One useful tool here is a simple chart with timescale at the top and emerging technologies on the left. When you first identify technology trends, put them up on the chart and sort them in order of relevance, based on timeframe or potential impact on your business. Then, based on your own findings, try to map when the technology is expected to have passed the hype phase as well as when it is expected to reach mainstream adoption having "crossed the chasm". As previously with information gathering, do not approach this believing that it will result in definite and precise answers. Rather, see this as an exercise with the goal of establishing a thought process and a better understanding of the world from a technological perspective. Over time, and probably also through cooperation with peers, this chart will ideally cover approximately 10 emerging technologies, and will evolve into a very useful tool for upcoming discussions on the future of business and technology.

ASSESS BUSINESS IMPLICATIONS

The next step in the Analyze – Assess – Adapt model is to assess how your shortlist of emerging technologies will affect your future business from different perspectives. Drawing inspiration from Henry Mintzberg, Michael Porter, Alexander Osterwalder, W Chan Kim and Renée Mauborgne, to mention but a few thought leaders in the area of competitive and strategic analysis, the goal with this hands-on guide is simplification. The aim is to introduce something that is easily accessed and possible to use in a hectic operative business environment. As discussed earlier, one should not believe that it is possible to get a full overview and understanding of the business implications of a new technology. Instead, this whole approach is aimed at creating a new mindset and overall understanding of the intersection of business and technology.

Emerging technologies have an impact in all areas of business, ranging from how an industry changes, to how customers react, to the inner workings of a company and new operational challenges and opportunities. Based on this, and in an attempt to simplify but not over simplify, we can list a total of nine areas that need to be considered:

From an industry perspective
Existing and new competition
Suppliers and collaborators
Standards and regulations
From a customer perspective
Value proposition
Products and services
Markets and segments
From a company perspective
People and processes
Marketing and sales
Procurement and production

Next comes making an assessment on the business implications of the new technology. How will this change the competition? How will this change client behavior? How will this change our internal processes?

Because of new innovations and applications, business model development can be both an opportunity and sometimes a necessity to fight the competition.

FROM AN INDUSTRY PERSPECTIVE

One of the very first and most important business issues relating to an emerging technology is how it will affect the **existing competitive landscape** in your industry. All companies have at least one, but often many, competitors, especially if you include different customer segments. It is therefore important to see how a technology will affect every different aspect of competition. How will your competitors react to new enabling technologies? Are they usually quick in adapting to the next big thing, or always late to the party? Are they innovative and likely to find new market opportunities coming out of the technology? All these things are essential perspectives, and highly relevant as part of a competitive technology assessment.

In the case of substitutes or **new, and sometimes unexpected, entrants**, it is important to assess most of the above aspects of competition. Also, new entrants can sometimes reap the benefits of simply being "new". They start from scratch, meaning no potential sunk costs in an existing organization, distribution network, infrastructure or traditions. Instead, a new entrant can attack with a fresh perspective, meaning they often come from industries that are familiar with relevant technologies and can put them to work in totally new settings in new industries. In this scenario, it is important to look for emerging competition in similar industries that have already adopted the new technology, or (much harder), try to spot signs of interest from previously distant industries.

> From a technology perspective, it is important to take part in discussions and to understand emerging standards and how these could affect competition or supplier strength.

When it comes to the technology perspective of **suppliers** as well as that of partners and **collaborators,** challenges and disruption often come from areas that were earlier considered "friendly". This has been seen in recent years, one very good example being the then CEO of Google Inc., Eric Schmidt, also serving on the board of Apple Inc. The companies collaborated in internet search, for example. Then when Apple launched the iPhone, and Google acquired the Android mobile OS, the partners suddenly became fierce competitors. With this in mind, be sure to stay informed about what your suppliers and partners are up to. Are they expanding their businesses into new areas fueled by technology?

Are they showing a sudden interest in what is happening in your part of the industry? Maybe they want to renegotiate a contract for no (initially) obvious reason? Are they hiring people with fundamentally new skill sets? From your company? As long as you stay informed and follow activities in the market, the chances are high that you can stay on top and ahead.

Standards and regulations are a sometimes strange combination of "good and evil". On the one hand, they provide stability, entry barriers and cost efficiencies in, for example, a production unit with standardized pallets or dimensions of raw material entering the facility. On the other hand, they limit flexibility for individual companies as well as for whole industries, sometimes creating inferior customer experiences.

From a technology perspective, it is important to take part in discussions and to understand emerging standards and how these could affect competition or supplier strength. As technology evolves, what new standards will emerge? With the introduction of a new technology, will the government enforce regulations? Is it possible to identify the different interest groups working on ways to change policies and regulations?

FROM A CUSTOMER PERSPECTIVE

The definition of a customer **value proposition** is that, in a convincing way, it explains why a customer should buy a product or service and also why the offering is superior to the competition. Traditionally, this superiority is either a price or quality advantage. There are also three types of customer value proposition. The *first* is a simple list of benefits the offering might deliver, the *second* is based on differentiation in relation to competing offerings and the *third* (and most favorable) is made up of the key points of difference with the greatest value to the customer. With this in mind, the fundamental question is, of course, whether an emerging technology will in any way change (or take away) any part of the value proposition that the customer finds most relevant.

There are a number of relevant perspectives where technology can change a value proposition.

The first and most essential question today is whether your fundamental product or service is becoming digital, and also whether there can be a relevant future combination of physical and digital products as well as offerings adding relevant services to existing products.

Imagine, for example, how mobile connectivity and social networks are changing customer service, and how a community of engaged users can vastly improve a company's service and support function. Also, the use of customer data and advanced analytics is essential when working with new value propositions.

With the increasing flow of new and improved digital tools, there are also new ways to approach the development of **products and services**. The first and most essential question today is whether your fundamental product or service is becoming digital, and also whether there can be a relevant future combination of physical and digital products as well as offerings adding relevant services to existing products. Do we have a good understanding of the customer's behavior, meaning do we know what they do and why, where and how they do it? New services can also be developed by expanding reach in mobile and social media, and while using customer data acquisition and analysis in new and innovative ways.

How will existing **markets and segments** change, and where will new market opportunities emerge? Will customers expect new and more tailored solutions, faster service or a lower price? To understand these parameters, you can assess new market opportunities and potentially interesting customer segments using digital methods to acquire relevant data through direct customer interaction, as well as from social media activities.

FROM A COMPANY PERSPECTIVE

In an organization, new technologies are always working their way into operations, **people and processes.** The trends here are very clear towards (for example) online broadband mobile technologies that let us work anywhere, anytime, often resulting in a demand for 24/7 availability from employers. For some, this is a good combination that creates freedom, but for others, this creates a constant conflict between work and life. That said, we can already see new ways of handling this, and as this technology enters the transformation phase, a relative balance will be found.

When we see new levels of white-collar automation and software assisted decision-making, what will happen to the role of the middle manager? Will new technology platforms provide quantum leaps in efficiency and cost reductions/ quality improvements that ensure your company stays competitive? It is worth stressing that operational excellence is a great competitive advantage since it is very hard for competitors to understand and copy the performance of an organization.

Emerging technologies and innovations are also changing the way in which companies handle their procurement and production.

INDUSTRY	
Existing and new competition	What are existing competitors doing, and are they early adopters or laggards?
	Are other industries already using this technology?
	Will we see new entrants into the industry?
Partners and collaborators	Will this give more power to our existing partners and/or collaborators?
	Will this give us new partners and/or collaborators?
	Are your partners and/or collaborators expanding into your area?
Standards and regulations	What new standards will emerge?
	Will new regulations emerge? New legal requirements?
	Who will lead this work? The government? Large industry players?
CUSTOMER	
Value proposition (and offering?)	What new value can you deliver to your customers? How can you deliver it?
	How will customer needs and expectations change?
	What parts of your existing value proposition will be less important or obsolete?
Products and services	Can your product or service be digitized and automated?
	Can you add products to your services or vice versa?
	Can the customer take part in the development and/or production of your offering?
Markets and segments	Are your markets or segments open to new innovations? Which are most affected?
	Can you take your offering to new markets or segments?
	Areas where you see high (even exponential) growth from low levels?
COMPANY	
People and processes	Will this change the way we organize work?
	What new competencies will we need? What old ones will disappear?
	Can this improve your operational excellence?
Marketing and sales	Will this improve understanding of your audience?
	Will this provide new ways of reaching and interacting with your customers?
	Will this change your branding and/or positioning?
Supply chain	Will this give more power to your existing suppliers?
	Moving up the value chain?
	Will this open up for new suppliers?
	Will this mean new production processes? Warehousing? Logistics? Other?

With new communication tools and social media, the customer is easy to reach and often willing to broadcast their opinions in an instant, which is regularly the case when a product or service does not meet expectations.

In marketing and sales, new technologies are rapidly changing the playing field. With new communication tools and social media, the customer is easy to reach and often willing to broadcast their opinions in an instant, which is regularly the case when a product or service does not meet expectations. With all communications, and often also transactions, happening at high speed, this creates new challenges for everyone in marketing and sales. What communication channels to use? What level of transparency to aim for?

Of course, all this communication and socialization also creates many opportunities. Today, there is less guesswork involved in targeting existing and potential customers with personalized advertising, and with data analytics tools it is possible to optimize the marketing budget.

Emerging technologies and innovations are also changing the way in which companies handle their **procurement and production**. With new and more efficient methods of communication, using large quantities of data, come improvements in all parts of the process, from software that can visualize and predict sufficient order volumes, to in-depth collaboration with all partners in the supply chain.

With innovations in manufacturing, for example more autonomous industrial robots and 3D printing, come new challenges and opportunities for any organization that handles physical goods. When should we use 3D printers for prototyping, and when will the technology be useful for large-scale manufacturing (if it is at all)? How could a company use software and data analytics to increase warehouse efficiency and at the same time limit back orders?

With these nine perspectives on how new technologies change the ways in which companies operate and interact with their environment, it is interesting to see that this all comes down to sometimes small, but often big, changes in existing business models. There are five different situations in which technology drives this reinvention.[79]

1. Reinventing industries, where a whole industry is transformed because of a new technology.
2. Substituting products or services, where digitalization replaces your existing offering.

3. Creating new digital businesses, where new technologies are creating (not replacing) products or services, thus adding revenues.
4. Reconfiguring value delivery models, where a company uses products, services and data in an innovative way to change the power balance within an industry value chain.
5. Rethinking value propositions, where new disruptive technologies are used to target customers or needs that are not met with existing offerings.

When discussing the intersection of technology and business model innovation, the "innovation

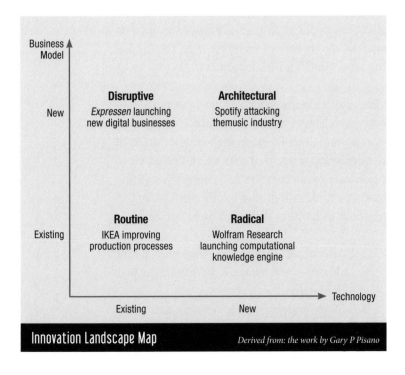

Innovation Landscape Map   *Derived from: the work by Gary P Pisano*

landscape map"[80] gives a very good overview of the innovation challenge based on two dimensions: the degree of technological change and the degree of business model change. The result is four categories of innovation:

Routine innovation, where existing technological competencies are combined with existing business models (and customer bases). IKEA serves as example, with a solid business model for the past 50 years, and with technology innovation and adaption according to needs in operations and also in customer interaction.

Disruptive innovation, where the innovation focus is on new business models while taking advantage of existing technology. The tabloid daily *Expressen* is a good example here, having successfully moved most of its focus to digital while still maintaining a rapidly declining print edition. Interesting here is that the publishers are also rapidly moving into technology innovation themselves, and not just trusting others to do this.

Radical innovation, where the innovation is only technological. Wolfram Research has been a very innovative software company for the past 30 years, and a highly successful innovator in the computation industry. Interesting here is that as the competitive landscape changes, and the app economy is emerging, Wolfram Research is experimenting with new, innovative business models.

> Often, disruptive innovation is only the starting point, and continuous, routine innovation is then necessary to fight off competition in the long run.

Architectural innovation, where a company engages in both business model and technology innovation. This is by far the most difficult quadrant for any company, especially for an incumbent with technological and organizational structures already in place. Starting in 2006, Spotify attacked the music industry with a radical new business model, "all you can eat" music subscription, and at the same time was first to offer a cloud-based music streaming service.

It is interesting to see where your own company is positioned. It is important to understand that all four quadrants can show equal growth potential, and different kinds of innovation should be seen as complements rather than substitutes. Often, disruptive innovation is only the starting point, and continuous, routine innovation is then necessary to fight off competition in the long run.

MERGING TECHNOLOGY ANALYSIS WITH BUSINESS ASSESSMENT

By using a radar analogy, it is possible to gain a simple and straightforward view of business implications. One radar image per technology is useful to get an overview. Map each business area (implication) on a scale from low to medium and high impact. Remember not to take the time perspective into account at this stage, concentrate on business implications for now.

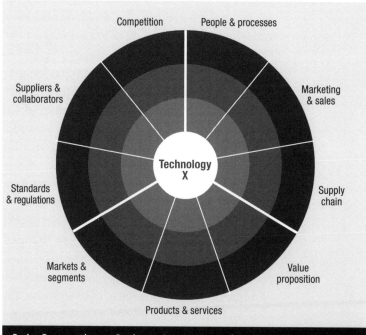

Radar Perspective on Business Assessment of Technology

Former US President Dwight D. Eisenhower was said to organize his workload and priorities according to two parameters.[81] These were "important", as in activities that have an outcome that leads to us achieving our goals, and "urgent", as in activities that need to be taken care of immediately. When put in a matrix, these two perspectives create a simple and powerful tool for time management.

The same analogy can be used in the analyze-assess-adapt model when considering technologies' impact on business. With what urgency should the technology be addressed, and how important is the impact on the future of the business?

By mapping each of the technologies according to levels of urgency and business impact, and plotting them in a matrix similar to the Eisenhower Principle, the result is a visual representation of the relative importance of each technology. Based on this tool, it is now easy to gain a good overview of the strategic technology landscape for your organization. By keeping it close at hand, you will have updated alerts as the business and technology environment changes.

So what we look at here are two perspectives of urgency and importance that will give the user four views of strategic technology priority. By mapping each individual technology from the two perspectives, it is easy to set priorities between technologies. Also, mapping progress over time gives trends on where and at what speed a specific technology is heading.

MEGATRENDS

TECHNOLOGIES

CASES

FRAMEWORK

EXECUTION

TECHSTORM 44

1. **Act**, when a technological threat or opportunity is imminent, and will have significant impact on your business environment. If you are not already embracing this technology, and unless you have a very good reason not to, now is the time to act.

2. **Prepare**. These are the technologies that you need to understand thoroughly and for which you need to plan once they take off.

3. **Monitor**. These technologies are, by definition, not relevant for your business – as of today, that is! As technology evolves and goes from experimentation through expansion and then eventually transforms society, the use and implications of a technology are bound to change.

4. **Watch**, when technology disruption is imminent but not relevant to your industry or business. That said; do not fully discard the technology, since the landscape might change rapidly.

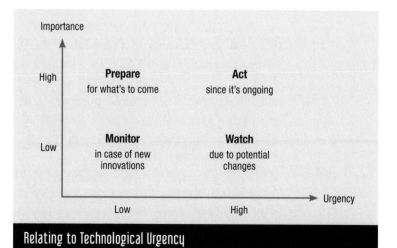

Relating to Technological Urgency

ADAPT TO UNCERTAINTY

In recent years, organizations have become more and more aware of the fact that "uncertainty is the new normal". It is likely that the business world we used to know, where strategic planning was simply extrapolating a trend, based on the past couple of years, has come to an end. Instead we see the emergence of a new understanding and acceptance of the fact that different perspectives on uncertainty and ambiguity are essential for future success.[82]

As with many other management approaches, this field has its roots in the military. In the 1990s, the acronym VUCA was introduced, short for vulnerability, uncertainty, complexity and ambiguity.[83] The original purpose of this approach was to address strategic foresight and insight as well as include a behavioral perspective on groups and individuals.

To give an overview of the field, consider the graph opposite[84] where the two perspectives are "understanding of the situation" and "predictability of your own actions". This will provide four alternative scenarios where the VUCA perspectives fit well.

- **Volatility**, a situation that is unstable and may be of unknown duration, but often with available information.
- **Complexity**, a situation with lots of variables, some predictable but the sheer scope of information is often overwhelming.
- **Uncertainty**, a situation with lack of information and unknown cause and effect. Unclear if the situation is stable.

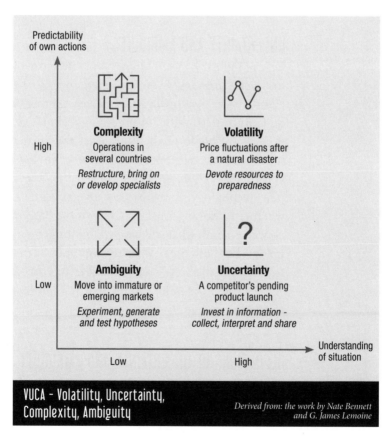

VUCA - Volatility, Uncertainty, Complexity, Ambiguity

Derived from: the work by Nate Bennett and G. James Lemoine

- **ambiguity**, a completely unclear situation with very limited (if any) information. Also the results of your actions are unclear.

With the above in mind, this section will deal with uncertainty and ambiguity, mainly because these are two of the most relevant perspectives when discussing emerging technologies from a strategic business perspective. Volatility and complexity are also of interest, but more relevant when your own actions are predictable, at least to some extent.

UNCERTAINTY AND AMBIGUITY

Every industry, technology, and investment involves a certain level of risk. Often, though, the exact level of risk involved in a given venture is quite uncertain. With any emerging technology, it is impossible to predict fully what the impact will be. This is true both of the new technology and of the technology being replaced. When a new technology develops and people choose whether or not to invest in it, one of the biggest concerns lies in what will happen to the old technology. For both the new technology and the old technology, there are many possible futures. It is with these potential futures that risk, uncertainty, and ambiguity come into play.

DEFINITIONS OF UNCERTAINTY AND AMBIGUITY

Although uncertainty and ambiguity overlap when it comes to investment decisions, there are clear distinctions between the two terms. The outcome of a sporting event is an example of uncertainty. While we may be able to calculate odds regarding which team will be victorious, this is not a clear cut case of probability. There is certainly risk involved in betting on a sporting match, but the probabilities of the potential outcomes are based on vague factors rather than known factors. Ambiguity refers to a specific type of uncertainty in which there are no clear beliefs regarding the probabilities of any given outcome.

THE RISK OF NEW TECHNOLOGY CAN BE CAUSED BY UNCERTAINTY

Part of the uncertainty involved in a new technology relates to the likelihood that it will succeed on its own, and on how quickly that success will occur. For any business dealing with the old technology, there will come a time when they have to make a decision to continue in their current direction, jump ship and invest in the new technology, or find a balance between the old and the new. Take the music industry, for example. When digital music and file sharing first made a big splash, record companies had to make a decision either to embrace the new technology or to continue to produce and release music in the ways it had done previously. While all companies struggled through this transition, the ones that embraced the newer technology and found a balance between both were the ones that succeeded best. Others held on to the old technology out of fear of the risk and uncertainty of the new.

While digital music is obviously at the forefront of the industry today, when it was first made available, there was plenty of uncertainty. How could anyone have known for sure that digital music would have such a drastic impact on the physical media? The outcome that occurred was one of many possible futures.

TO INVEST OR NOT TO INVEST?

Risk falls when the known probability that something will happen increases, but waiting too long to make an investment could also result in less profit. As the adage goes, the more you risk, the greater the potential reward. The risk involved in an investment relates directly to the probability of any given future and indirectly to the uncertainty that is inherent in anything still in the development stages. The simple fact is that no one is certain that a new technology will "work." It may function as it is intended, but will it actually work in the sense that society will adopt it?

Investing in new technology often involves a relatively short-term risk that blossoms into a long-term reward. It may take months or years before this technology pays off. In the mean time, profits may be minimal or non-existent. However, if the technology does in fact take off and boom in a way that complements the investment strategy, then the long term reward will be plentiful. Of course, if the new technology flops, then the loss increases exponentially.

Investing in the old technology, on the other hand, often produces more of a long-term risk and a short-term reward. As the new technology waits in the wings while society makes its judgment, the old technology may even get a boost. There is often a mentality of gobbling up what we think we might not be able to have any more. However, if the new technology succeeds, the business may fail because it waited too long to invest. Of course, that does not mean that every new technology is a wise investment.

AMBIGUITY

There is also a sense of ambiguity with any emerging technology. It is often unclear exactly what the new technology is and where it might go, which will lead to potential futures that are almost impossible to predict. There is a basic understanding of that technology, but there are many questions about where it will overlap and how exactly it will be used in the future. We may be able to predict futures based on the information available, but there is no way to determine the probability that some of these particular futures will occur. The only thing known is that these futures are possible, or at least we think they are.

When a new technology emerges, the existing technology may not be rendered obsolete. Therefore, choosing to invest entirely in one technology or another may not be the only avenue available. Without a firm understanding of the long-term success and effect of the new technology, it may be difficult to make a full commitment.

> During the course of any business' life, there will inevitably be new technologies that present uncertainty about the future of both that company and the industry as a whole.

STRATEGIC UNCERTAINTY

Every business, or at least every business that wishes to succeed, routinely implements strategies in order to ensure growth and stability. Market research, competitor analysis, and other traditional tools can help a business create a strategy. However, these traditional tools are only effective when the business environment and economy are facing stable conditions. In today's rapidly developing world, this is hardly the case. Today, technological uncertainty is a major issue that all businesses must face. Therefore, strategic uncertainty has become a necessary factor in order for a business to survive ultimately.

Any new and developing technology creates some level of uncertainty. With a new technology, there are often many different futures for which to prepare. Planning for this uncertainty involves using the right tools to create the right strategy. When probabilities are unknown, creating an investment or business strategy requires innovative thinking. When planning in uncertain conditions, there are many factors that must be considered. In order for a business venture to succeed, resources have to be put into the right areas. A solid strategy in uncertain conditions takes forward thinking, the right tools, and the smartest moves.

DEALING WITH UNCERTAINTY AND SURVIVING DISRUPTION

Strategy under uncertain conditions essentially involves three basic steps: determining strategic options, selecting a strategic posture, and building a portfolio of strategic moves.[85] These steps require a thorough analysis of the potential futures, the goals of the company, and the types of moves that can get the company to that point. Of course, in order to deal with uncertainty, one first must gain some idea of the factors involved. In other words, one must determine as much as possible about the uncertain conditions. This may sound on paper like an exercise in futility, but it is a rational process that allows for real strategic thinking and action.

During the course of any business' life, there will inevitably be new technologies that present uncertainty about the future of both that company and the industry as a whole. Therefore it is important to determine the level of uncertainty involved and to plan how to deal with these technologies that can present a missed opportunity for the current business model.[86]

DETERMINING THE LEVEL OF UNCERTAINTY

No matter how uncertain a business environment may be, it is typically possible to identify trends that will help to determine more clearly potential future demand. There are also often unknown factors that can become known with the right analysis. While it may be impossible to know everything, using current data on similar technologies may help make things more certain. Even after analysis, there is bound to be some uncertainty, which falls into one of four levels: a single future, alternate futures, a range of futures, and true ambiguity.

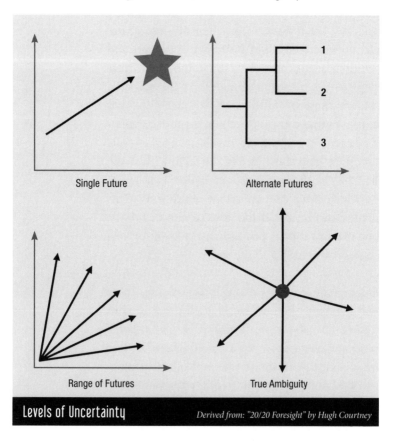

Single Future

Alternate Futures

Range of Futures

True Ambiguity

Levels of Uncertainty   *Derived from: "20/20 Foresight" by Hugh Courtney*

In at least half of all cases, there will be multiple future scenarios for which to plan.[87] There may be instances where one future seems far more likely than others, and planning for only one future may work in these instances. However, new technologies are rarely this predictable. Instead, most new technologies will fall into one of two categories: "only a few futures" or "a wide range of futures".

Regardless of the number of futures that seem possible, a business must use the appropriate analytic tools to find the right strategies. Knowing the number of futures is important because it will help shape the types of tools a business uses. While it is not necessary to come up with an exact number of futures, one must be able to gauge the difference between a few and many possibilities.

THE RIGHT STRATEGIC POSTURE

Figuring out how to analyze for the type of uncertainty faced is only the first step, but it is certainly an important step. Whenever uncertainty is involved, the strategic thinking must be flexible and tailored to the level of uncertainty.[88] A one-size-fits-all approach will often render a plan unresponsive and result in failure.

Once the right approach is used to analyze the uncertainty, it is time to select the right strategic posture. The term "posture" refers to the intent of the strategy as it relates to the current and future states of the industry. When trying to combat uncertainty, there are two different strategic postures that are available for a business to adopt: shaping and adapting. Before developing the actual strategy, it is necessary to choose which posture or intent to use.

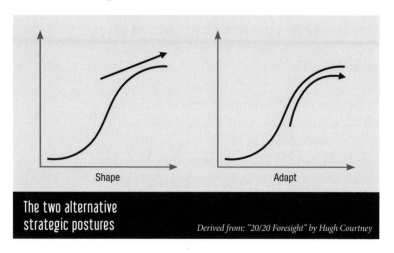

The two alternative strategic postures

Derived from: "20/20 Foresight" by Hugh Courtney

The strategic posture of shaping will be adopted by companies looking to shape the future. In other words, this posture is selected by those companies looking to be a leader in the industry. With this posture, the intent is to drive the industry forward and establish new ways of operating. Shapers look to create new opportunities by shaking up the current status quo of the industry or by attempting to control the areas where the market is uncertain. By investing heavily in digital photography in the late 1990s, Kodak demonstrated that its preferred strategic posture, at least in this particular instance, was shaping. Shapers often hold the opinion that the best way to survive a new technology is to develop their own disruption to the industry before it is too late.[89]

A second strategic posture is adapting. When using this posture, the intent is to adapt to how the future will be shaped. Rather than pushing forward a new technology, this posture relies on watching the industry carefully and taking advantage of existing opportunities. This is a reactive rather than a proactive strategy, and it depends on quick responses in order to work. An example of adaptation can be seen in Barnes and Noble's decision to implement its own e-reader in response to the dominance of Amazon's Kindle and e-book sales.[90] This decision to respond to the changing market allowed Barnes and Noble to survive while other bricks and mortar book stores did not, at least for the time being.

CREATING THE STRATEGY PORTFOLIO

Having a strategic posture is not in itself an answer to any new investment, technology, or other uncertainty. The posture is just a skeleton of a strategy. It does not provide any methods or actions by which a business can reach its aims. Once the posture is determined, usually corresponding to the level of uncertainty, then a portfolio of actions is the next move.

There are three types of moves that are most relevant to implementing a strategy when conditions are uncertain: big bets, options, and no regrets moves.[91] A portfolio may only consist of one type of move, or it may use more than one. Regardless of the different types of moves, it is important to have more than one option available.

Big bets, as suggested by the name, are major investments or other moves that will typically result either in large payoffs or significant losses. Most companies using the shaping posture will include big bets within the strategic portfolio. These moves are often not utilized in the other two postures.

The next type of move for the strategy portfolio consists of options. These moves are designed to yield big payoffs in best-case scenarios, while minimizing losses in worst cases. Options typically seem far less risky than big bets, and they allow a company to make modest investments up front while still affording the opportunity to make big investments later on. As one might expect, options are typically used by adapters. Since they allow for more time before making the investment, options usually work well.

No regrets moves are ones that are designed to pay off no matter what. Regardless of the outcome, these decisions will have positive payoffs. The payoffs might not be huge, but they minimize risk while still providing a guaranteed gain. Reducing costs and building skills are obvious no regrets moves that will produce a positive result in the end, no matter what happens.

Creating a strategy portfolio is highly dependent on the level of uncertainty a business is facing. Each step of strategic uncertainty is interconnected, and it is vital to go through each step thoroughly before attempting to implement any strategy.

PLANNING FOR UNCERTAINTY

Today's markets and technologies are too volatile for traditional business planning. In order to plan for uncertainty, a business has to rely on some innovation. Planning for uncertainty is not about trying to guess the one outcome that will occur. Rather, it is about being prepared for multiple outcomes while trying to create an understanding of how likely each outcome is. By looking at the most predictable elements of an industry or technology, it may be possible to reduce some uncertainty.

The right strategic planning takes an approach that evaluates uncertainty thoroughly before choosing the tools or moves that a business will make. No matter what tools you use or what moves are in your portfolio, you must be willing to adapt to changes in the industry. If you are not aware of how the future is shaping up, then you will not be able to respond quickly enough for your strategy to have a chance.

MEGATRENDS

TECHNOLOGIES

CASES

FRAMEWORK

EXECUTION

TECHSTORM 44

EXECUTE
IN TIMES OF
UNCERTAINTY

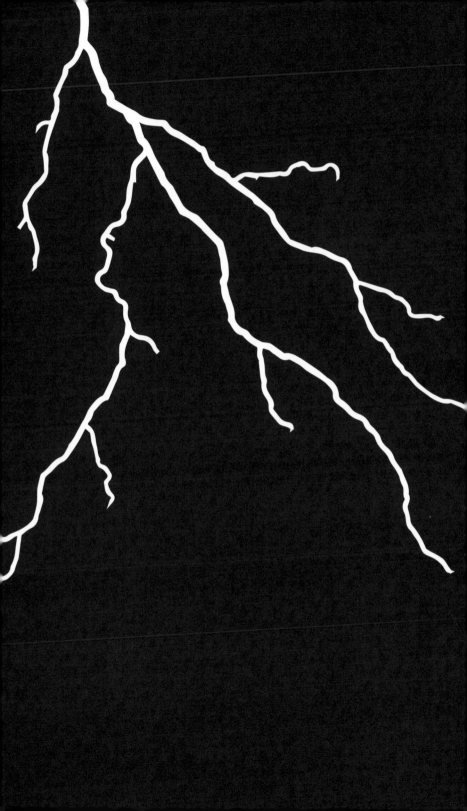

In today's world, there are few things that can be considered constants. There is a reason the saying about change being the only constant is quoted so often. Every major change brings us into a time of uncertainty, fear, and, at times, pure chaos. The fact that technology has advanced so rapidly in the past 50 years means that we are almost always reinventing the status quo. Today's smartphones are faster and more powerful than top of the range computers were a mere two decades ago. It is more than the fact that we have new gadgets to play with – we have to continue to determine how to use this new technology ethically, something that is often heavily debated. Without some guiding principles in place, we only add to the chaos.[92]

We will look at four different key areas that will help us work through the uncertainty created by technology and by other, more traditional forms of uncertainty. These areas include leadership, innovation, organization, and sustainability. While each area can be tackled on its own, the four cannot truly be separated: in order for a business to survive periods of uncertainty, all four of these areas must be addressed.

MEGATRENDS

TECHNOLOGIES

CASES

FRAMEWORK

EXECUTION

TECHSTORM 44

LEADING IN TIMES OF UNCERTAINTY

During times of uncertainty we truly see what our leaders are capable of doing. In 2008, the recession showed that some business leaders simply didn't know how to handle a crisis of that magnitude. Even those who did lead their companies through the recession and out the other side in relatively good shape found themselves questioning their decisions and their ability to handle future disasters. The fact is that no one can see the future, but it is still possible to plan for a crisis. Scenario planning has been used by the army since the 1950s[93], and many businesses and other organizations have adapted this type of crisis planning. However, even with these scenarios, there is always a chance that something unexpected will occur.

How can our leaders better prepare themselves to face uncertainly and the chaos that comes with it? There are a few different ways that have been used in the past to direct a business, organization, or even a government successfully during times of chaos.

CREATING ROLES

One of the most important aspects of any organization is the role played by each constituent member. This can (again) be seen clearly in the military, where every rank and position has specific duties. In a business, there may be a single leader in the CEO or board chairman, but rarely does this single individual control every aspect of the company. Leadership is decentralized. This provides a resilience to the business that makes it much easier to deal with uncertainty and with negative consequences[94], especially true in today's global market. It is difficult, if not impossible, for a CEO in China to be fully aware of the situation in the corporation's North American branch. By allowing different divisions of the company to have their own leaders and their own leadership models, these leaders have more freedom to respond to unexpected events.

Of course, decentralization does not mean each division is an island unto itself. It does not create a company made up of independent smaller companies. Coordinated decentralization is a resilient, strong way of dealing with uncertainty, as long as the various divisions communicate and work together towards common goals and follow common principles. When they do not, the leaders are not leading effectively.

STABILITY, NOT AGILITY

Some businesses, such as hedge funds, can move into and out of markets very quickly. They are stable yet very agile, able to drop a whole market in an instant. This gave some leaders the idea that being an agile business was the way to go.[95] However, this might set up the business to fail. Very few companies can change their direction that quickly, especially when they have gone to great lengths to establish their presence in a market. Purchasing office or factory space, providing the paperwork to operate in that area, and hiring employees, makes it very difficult simply to pull up roots and leave.

It also creates a negative reputation for the company. Pulling out of a market does not mean simply leaving the consumer without the products or services the company provides. It also means laying off employees and removing the income the company brought to the community. This is bound to make the business look bad in the eyes of many. A strong leader is going to know how to move the company in the right ways while maintaining relationships or, in times when hard choices have to be made, will take into account how decisions affect more than just their business, also a form of agility.

BATTLING AGAINST TRADITION

In times of uncertainty, it is easy to fall back on tradition: "This is how it's always been done, and since that's always worked, let's keep doing it!"[96] Those who are poor leaders will often cite tradition as the reasoning behind their decisions, and they will pull out a number of examples to back up their theory. However, as mentioned earlier, technology is changing so quickly and affecting so much that it is hard to apply any previous case to today's world. Taking a single event or activity out of the context and applying a traditional approach is setting up the business to fail.

One of the biggest "traditional" methods of success that today's leaders must learn to work against is the idea that a business must always try to grow and expand. Trying to expand simply for the sake of expanding is actually very counterproductive.[97] Instead, leaders have to recognize that no business can grow successfully without a very stable foundation. This is especially true in times of uncertainty. Even businesses that are not trying to expand may fail during these chaotic periods because they are not stable enough. Trying to expand while in a period of uncertainty can lead to a wide number of consequences that will damage the business in many different ways and could even lead to its total collapse.

All businesses will reach a point where they have to take risks or become stagnant. That is inevitable.

Of course, all businesses will reach a point where they have to take risks or become stagnant. That is inevitable. However, a good leader will know when to take a risk and when to hold back. Here is an area in which technology can help leaders make a more informed decision even if it has created the uncertainty that's threatening the business. Models, gathered data, and the ability to create dynamic scenarios all assist leaders, as does the fact that the business is decentralized. Those that follow the idea of decentralized leadership will be able to take more risks because the majority of the business will be protected. Even if a division of the company fails, it is only a setback, not a total defeat.

UNDERSTANDING THE ROLE OF TECHNOLOGY

The idea of becoming a leader, who successfully deploys technology to bring about stability and transformation, is relatively new.[98] However, being a digital master can make a business more profitable than its competitors. The thinking encompasses a number of different points, but one of the main ideas is meshing the past with the present and the future. This goes back to learning from traditional approaches, but also being wise enough to know when those approaches are going to fail because the context is different.

Those who become successful leaders in today's technological world have to have a vision for where they want their company to go. This is more than simply coming up with a marketing plan or saying that the business should bring in a specific amount of money by the end of the year. It's about having an understanding of technology, clear intentions and specific, measurable outcomes. It is also about evolving. While a business must have a stable foundation from which to build, it must also be flexible and ready to make changes. A good leader knows that his or her vision for the company needs to evolve as the world changes in order to survive in times of uncertainty.

Engagement is another important aspect of leading in the digital community. Leaders know how to engage their employees with, and through, technology. Today's technology gives every employee a voice through social networking and other ways of connecting. This, in turn, allows leaders to hear what their employees want and

A strong leader who has a vision, engages employees, builds a stable foundation for the company, and knows when to take risks, may still have to struggle in times of uncertainty, but will be equipped with the tools needed to guide the business through them.

need. Executives who are consistent in their communication and maintain an open, ongoing dialogue will not just be a boss, they will be an active leader who has a workforce that feels valued and truly wants to do the best work possible.[99]

BEING A GOOD LEADER IN TIMES OF UNCERTAINTY

The overall takeaway from this is that leading during a time of uncertainty is by no means easy, but it also does not have to mean leading from a position of weakness, fear, or pure reaction. A strong leader who has a vision, engages employees, builds a stable foundation for the company, and knows when to take risks, may still have to struggle in times of uncertainty, but will be equipped with the tools needed to guide the business through them. Those who simply retreat to their offices and hope that everything will work out for the best will find themselves captaining a sinking ship.

LEADERSHIP TOOLBOX

In a situation where uncertainty is the new norm, lots of pressure is put on the leader of an organization. Again, looking at leadership in a VUCA environment, Colonel Eric G. Kail, artillery officer with three combat tours, a Ph.D. in organizational psychology and now course director for military leadership at West Point, gets straight to the point with addressing leadership challenges from a VUCA perspective in a series of posts on www.hbr.org.

Three ways to lead more effectively in a volatile environment:
1. Ask your team to translate data into information
Focus all communication on the right, usable information, not raw data that the receiver has to analyze and extract.
2. Communicate clearly
Get rid of the buzz words and one-liners. Be clear, concise and straight to the point.
3. Ensure your intent is understood
If your intent is clear, then your team will be able to handle volatile situations by themselves.

Three ways to lead more effectively in an uncertain environment:
1. Get a fresh perspective
Challenge your individual and collective perceptions, preferably by using a devil's advocate. Make sure you rotate this role in your team.
2. Be flexible
Have a strategy and operational plan, but include flexibility and options to handle an uncertain reality.
3. Glance back, look ahead
Focus on what you can do better in the future, not what you did wrong in the past.

Three ways to lead more effectively in a complex environment:

1. Develop collaborative leaders

Make sure that your co-workers see the big picture and value in a collaborative mindset.

2. Stop seeking permanent solutions

In complex environments, focus must never be on finding a 100% solution to a problem, as then you will miss other opportunities.

3. Train tomorrow's heroes now

Set aside the proper resources to develop young leaders. Successful in-house talent development is a necessity in any organization.

Three ways to lead more effectively in an ambiguous environment:

1. Listen well

Someone asking, "What's our goal?" is signaling that you need to be clear in your communication. Do not just hear what you want to hear.

2. Think divergently

Be open to new ideas, and realize that, in an ambiguous environment, there is not only one best solution to a problem.

3. Set up incremental dividends

It is hard to celebrate reaching milestones in an ambiguous environment, but it is an important way to build and maintain momentum.

INNOVATE IN TIMES OF UNCERTAINTY

Next, let us look at another key factor in surviving and thriving in times of uncertainty: innovation. This occurs all the time: people discover a new way of doing something that is truly innovative and leads to a revolution in that industry. However, during times of uncertainty, innovation often occurs more out of necessity, and less as a result of simple experimentation or from a desire to learn and grow. Survival prompts this type of innovation, and while it is certainly no better or worse than innovation that occurs during periods of stability, it is often more focused. People are looking for ways to combat specific threats and issues, and that may lead to very tight innovation in some industries, with some possibilities going completely ignored.

Innovation does not happen in a bubble, nor can it happen when the right tools are absent. It can be difficult for large, well established businesses to innovate because, as mentioned earlier, their leaders become so entrenched in tradition that they do not allow for what they see as disruptive ideas to enter the conversation. It is these disruptive ideas, however, that often lead to innovative solutions to age-old problems.

IT STARTS AT THE TOP

As with almost all things, innovation starts at the top. A few random middle managers or a small department may, at one point or another, have an innovative breakthrough, but this is far, far less likely to happen in an organization where the leaders do not actively encourage innovation. The successful managers in a rapidly changing technological environment are actually also innovation masters. They have all the right tools to inspire others. They use technology to connect the organization in ways that businesses have not been connected before.

But this has to extend beyond simply talking to one another. An innovative leader will use an innovative business model, fighting against the traditional idea of every division working on its own. Instead, he or she will encourage open collaboration, communication, and the free exchange of ideas.[100] Such leaders encourage their workers not to just do their jobs, but to look at themselves as entrepreneurs. Many are surprised by what happens when an employee is given the freedom to look beyond his or her job description. 3M and Google are examples of two companies where employees are encouraged to spend part of their time pursuing ideas outside their work description, clearly fostering an innovative environment.

This culture of communication often results in ideas falling into the laps of those who would never otherwise have heard them. For example, the engineering division may casually mention a new project to someone in accounting. As an outsider to the department, this accountant may have insight that makes the engineers realize that what they are building is biased towards the end user seeing the world as an engineer would. This, in turn, leads to a major change in the product that makes it much more innovative and useful to the general public.

This free exchange of ideas can only occur if a strong leader and their company culture fosters the idea of open communication and collaboration

There can be no true innovation without understanding that innovation does not happen in a vacuum. The environment is one of the biggest factors in innovation, especially the technological environment.

where everyone is treated as an equal. In companies where this does not exist, far too often the hierarchy of the business kills innovation. Job titles are given too much weight, leaving a low level employee afraid to speak his or her mind. This kills collaboration and leads to some feeling less valued than others. A good leader will make certain that there are methods in place that allow all ideas to be heard and acted upon. The leader will even be willing to improvise from time to time, especially when things are uncertain.[101]

But a good leader is not the only thing required for innovation. The best leader in the world will find it difficult to encourage innovation without the proper tools and mindset in place.

AGAIN, CONTEXT IS IMPORTANT

There can be no true innovation without understanding that innovation does not happen in a vacuum. The environment is one of the biggest factors in innovation, especially the technological environment.[102] Social media, mobile devices, and many other technologies we now use every day have reshaped our environment. What was once an innovative idea in a world in which people were not connected 24/7, is now useless. The rules of business, information, entertainment, and, in many ways, of simply going about a daily routine, have been so changed that technology has become less of a factor in innovative thinking and more of a constant, omnipresent presence.

BUT IT IS ALSO A HINDRANCE

Conversely, context can also hold back innovation. Like traditional approaches, context can so dominate the way people approach a problem that it actually holds back innovation. People get so caught up in budgets, visions, priorities, resource management and more that they fail to see something that should be very obvious. Trying to juggle all the company's goals, while framing everything within the context in which the company operates, can lead to creating a very small box in which to operate. Very little innovation can be done in such a box.

That is why it is a great idea to sit down periodically and figuratively wipe everything away.[103] There is a need to take a look at the big picture without worrying about how the company fits into it, or how the context affects you. Look at trends, recent innovative ideas, and how the industry is growing and changing. Look at this environment as a whole and see where it's going. Often, the best innovations are those that build upon what is already there or step in to fill a noticeable gap.

APPROACH THREATS HEAD ON

One area that often drives innovation is the area of threat response. A good leader with a vision will find that their goals and plans for the future often fizzle out or, worse, hit a brick wall face first if they do not have plans for when things go horribly wrong. The threat response involves doing what unnerves many people: looking at worse case scenarios head on. The idea of addressing these threats and drastic outcomes as something that can occur forces people to think of the outcomes, and they are rarely comforting. However, by coming at these threats head on and devising solutions for each, the business becomes more stable and more adaptable.

The process leads to innovative ideas being thrown around. How does one approach a certain situation that seems to have no solution? The answer is: by creating a solution. Preparing to deal with doomsday scenarios is not just about being prepared – it is about being prepared to handle the situation in the most effective, least disruptive way possible. That often means it is time to create something new.

AVOID BANDWAGONS

"All our competitors are doing this. We're going to be left behind if we don't!" This type of thinking leads to businesses jumping onto bandwagons after that initial innovative idea hits the market and dominates it. While there is definitely money to be made in following on the heels of an innovation by refining it and creating more perfect versions, that is not true of innovation, and more often than not, the attempt results in creating an inferior version that only serves to cost the company money. For example, how many small music players other than the iPod were out there? Most people cannot name any other brand, or if they can, it is a brand that has failed or controls very little of the market. That said, remember that the unique innovation behind the iPod was not necessarily the player itself, rather the ecosystem combining the player with the iTunes music store.

Instead of leaping from big idea to big idea, innovative companies look at the basic idea behind the innovation. Could it be taken in another direction? Is there a key technology or idea there that can be used in other ways? Why is this innovation so popular now, and what does that popularity tell us? Take a good, hard look at the innovation, and then look beyond it. It has been suggested that almost all great innovations are driven by one of three things[104]:

- creating a business model that makes money

- creating a solution to a problem

- creating a technology that allows a solution to be implemented

When innovation comes from the intersection of two or all three of these things, it tends to shatter barriers and quickly go from the newest thing to the status quo very quickly.

In times of uncertainty, it feels much safer to grab on to something successful and try to run with it, even if someone else is doing it better. But by slowing down, examining the innovation, and making it your own, you will actually come out better in the end and you will stand out as a leader, not another follower.

DO NOT LET PLANNING KILL INNOVATION

Paperwork is almost universally reviled, and there are reasons for this: it is tedious, it is boring, and it seems as if it only creates more paperwork. It can also kill innovation, especially if the red tape becomes so thick that any new idea takes months to go through the approval phase. The last thing any leader should do is implement so much bureaucracy that innovative ideas never become more than ideas. Yes, business plans, outlines, book-keeping and other documents are certainly important, but planning should never stand in the way of creating. This also goes back to what it takes to be a good leader in a world of uncertainty: the willingness to set aside meticulous planning and simply let people try things out. Otherwise, the long march through the approval process may kill the project's momentum and the innovator's drive to create it.

The key that many top innovative businesses follow is simple: less paperwork, more testing and demo creation.[105] That is not to say that there should not be documented plans or concepts, but being able to say that the technology or methodology needed to create something can be done and then show a working model is worth so much more. One interesting approach to this is the "build – measure – learn" methodology from the lean startup movement, also useful in a general innovation perspective.

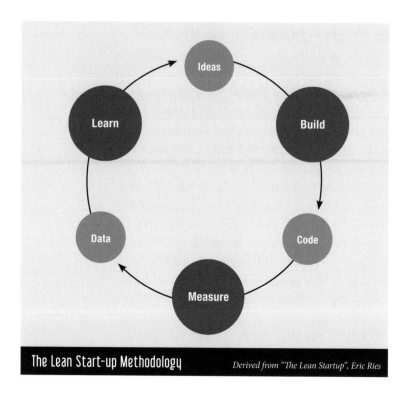

The Lean Start-up Methodology   *Derived from "The Lean Startup", Eric Ries*

INNOVATE YOURSELF TO CERTAINTY

Businesses trapped in a time of uncertainty can escape through innovation by creating new solutions to the problems they are facing. By providing strong leadership that allows for innovation through cooperation, a business will be able to meet its challenges head on and defeat them.

INNOVATION TOOLBOX

In "The Myths of Innovation", Scott Berkun debunks generic innovations myths and, among other things, presents five challenges for managing innovation:

Life of Ideas

The life of an idea is worth nothing if the idea is not taken forward; the important thing is what you do with it. The nurturing of ideas is the responsibility and an important trait of a great leader. By encouraging discussions and heated debates, demos, prototyping and the occasional failure, you develop an environment where creativity is the norm. From this, crazy and sometimes useless ideas will emerge, but with an open discussion these will be sorted out and the great ones will survive.

Environment

The generation of ideas and level of innovation is closely related to the environment in which an organization is working. This goes both for the physical environment with an office that nurtures discussions and random interactions as well as for the atmosphere and corporate culture. Is it OK to question the ideas coming from a superior? Also, this goes hand in hand with recruitment efforts. To establish a creative environment, you must have creative, imaginative and self-driven people who can challenge existing behaviors and preconceived beliefs.

Protection

Another very important innovation trait found with successful managers is that they provide protection for their team. Having the ability to focus on the tasks at hand without having to attend to shareholders, media, customers, budgets or office politics is essential in any creative process. Also, when the innovation is being turned into a product or service, it is the responsibility of the leader to push towards a deadline without pushing the team too far.

Execution

Innovation is time consuming and difficult, but execution on an idea is the most difficult part of the process. In a creative process, it is necessary and somewhat of a luxury not having to deal with all the minuscule details. When shipping a product or service, everything has to be taken care of, including the less relevant parts of the innovation. Here the innovators must often also face reality and compromise, and it is in situations like this that great leaders excel.

Persuasion

So when the idea is there, the target group identified and the product development project is underway, innovation team leaders face another challenge: The act of persuasion. It is not enough to protect the team from red tape and budget constraints, the leader must also convince various stake holders such as share holders, venture capitalists and banks, for funding. This is a very challenging environment where everyone involved must be able to handle multiple rejections. The most important success factors here are believing in your idea and being persistent.

MEGATRENDS //// TECHNOLOGIES ///// CASES ///// FRAMEWORK ///// **EXECUTION** ///////// TECHSTORM 44 //////

ORGANIZE IN TIMES OF UNCERTAINTY

There are many challenges to innovation, of course, and one such challenge is disorganization. It can be difficult, if not impossible, to create any solutions when a company is so disorganized that its leaders and employees have to devote time and energy to finding information and resources instead of using that time to innovate and problem solve. However, in times of uncertainty, there is more to it: even the most organized business may find itself in need of reorganization. New technology, new problems, and new innovations can lead to the need to reorganize. Many once saw reorganization as a last ditch effort before a business failed completely, but that is no longer the case. Successful businesses led by strong leaders know that reorganization is sometimes necessary, and it is becoming more and more typical as a form of response to global trends and emerging technologies.[106]

REORGANIZING THE RIGHT WAY

The average term for a CEO of a worldwide company is only about five years.[106] That leaves very little time to establish much of anything resembling stability, and it means that he or she is only going to get the chance to reorganize the company once. This is especially true if the reorganization does not go well – shareholders and boards are quick to place the blame on the top executive and send them packing, even if the major issues were out of their control.

How can a leader go about reorganization in the right way in order to outlive the average lifespan of a global CEO? There is no easy answer to this question – every reorganization is going to be different. There are some similarities between those who have successfully reorganized, however.

The first thing to do is to address the problem. What is holding the company back? Why is this reorganization necessary? What does the company need more of, and what does it have too much of? Answering these questions allows the leader to create a framework for the reorganization.

How can a leader go about reorganization in the right way in order to outlive the average lifespan of a global CEO?

This framework includes tangible elements like information, resources, and structure, along with intangible elements like motivators, commitments, and mindsets.[106] Both have to be considered when preparing to reorganize.

Building this framework is going to take time, and it is not as simple as creating jobs and plugging people into them. In fact, that is the exact idea that can lead to a business failing, especially during periods of uncertainty where the wrong leadership can be disastrous.

THE END OF WORKERS, THE BEGINNING OF PROBLEM SOLVERS

That is why a good leader does not look for workers – he or she looks for problem solvers, those who are innovative and maybe even have an entrepreneurial spirit that pushes them not only to show up from nine to five every day but to also step up and take ownership of their work. The idea is to create problem solvers or "thought leaders" – people who are creative, innovative, influential, and willing to go out of their way to make a business succeed.[109] These problem solvers are not afraid to share their ideas, get involved with large projects, and build up others. A worker, on the other hand, may feel as if they ought to be compensated for their thoughts, may have no drive to volunteer for anything, or feel so small that they have nothing to contribute.

That is not to say that everyone will be in a position to be innovative, but no one should ever feel like "just" a worker. Each employee needs to feel valued and needs to know that they do contribute to the overall objectives, goals, and community of the business.

A strong leader also has to realize that it takes more than simply telling someone they need to contribute – they have to show it. The atmosphere and environment is one of the things that a strong leader can control and can directly influence during reorganization. Putting forth the effort needed to make everyone part of the team isn't wasted time – it may not be directly measurable, but the intangible element of job satisfaction is one of the most important aspects of any business.

EVERYONE IS A KNOWLEDGE WORKER

A knowledge worker is someone who uses information every day, hopefully in a creative, innovative way. Often, knowledge workers are thought of as the creative people in a business.[110] Engineers, programmers, researchers, scientists, and others who create or sift through information are thought of as being more important than those who do more physical tasks. Assembly line personnel, janitorial staff, drivers, construction workers, and others are often considered as not just less important to a business but also as less educated and less valuable.

This point of view is one of those traditional things about which strong leaders are more than just aware; they are also aware that they must change this type of thinking. In today's world, everyone makes use of information in one way or another. Even those who follow the same basic routine every day, such as an assembly line worker, still have to be prepared to improvise and respond to unforeseen circumstances. With more and more reliance on technology, employees are not simply nailing something together. They are using expensive machinery to solder microchips or weld metal frames. This involves specialized training on the machinery used and on the overall computer system the business has. Even clocking in and out is done electronically now, and company memos are distributed through email rather than paper copies.

Everyone now uses information in some way in their everyday work lives. Everyone is, to some extent, a knowledge worker who can be innovative. When organizing a company or a department, a good leader will take this into consideration.

STEPPING OUTSIDE THE BOX

It's a horribly overused cliché, but the idea of stepping outside the box does still have some relevance. A new, novel approach to business is vital in a time of uncertainty, but this adaptive thinking has to go beyond company leadership – it has to reach the average employee. Your knowledge workers need to be able to approach situations with new adaptive thinking. This goes hand in hand with the above point that everyone uses technology now. It is not enough

> # Even those who are not comfortable with technology will need to be ready to step outside their comfort zones.

to understand a basic task – an employee now has to understand how to handle the technology that makes each basic task possible.

The rise of integrated computer networks and new communication technologies are certainly some of the main drivers of uncertainty[111], which is why it is important for employees to be prepared to deal with technological failures. Being literate in new media, a term used to describe social media, online culture, and the new forms of communication used daily, is vital to everyone in today's workforce. Even those who are not comfortable with technology will need to be ready to step outside their comfort zones.

This is one area where a leader can organize the company with an eye towards skill set, commitment, and accountability. Because it is a reorganization, leaders should not feel tied to the past. Putting those who have the right skills and knowledge into the right positions is key to any reorganization, but it is also key to put those willing to learn into positions where they can grow. Allowing each person to take ownership of their work and be accountable for it without feeling micromanaged is a key part of any business structure.[112]

ORGANIZING FOR THE FUTURE

Organizing a business, or reorganizing one, requires leaders to be willing to make changes not just for the duration of a chaotic, uncertain period, but also for the future. If the dust settles and stability returns will the business be in a position to function, or will it still be in combat mode, still ready to battle the problems it has been facing? Creating a flexible structure that can handle a variety of problems is difficult, but the key to everything is the people involved. With the right people in the right positions with the right sense of being valued, the rest of the organization will fall into place.

ORGANIZATION TOOLBOX

In times of new technological paradigms, when one technology wave is maturing and another is about to take over, new ideas for organization and cooperation are flourishing. Throughout this book, simplicity has been one of the guiding principles, and although the organization of a project or a company is never simple, the basic ideas should be.

One of the most interesting recent initiatives in this area is presented by the NOBL Collective (www.flox.works). Their idea is that the work of organizing should never overshadow the actual work, obvious but seldom understood. Their research shows that this leads to improvements in decision making, product delivery and overall profitability. Also, research shows vastly improved employee engagement in just 30 days when using this approach to working and organizing.

The method is based on **two habits** and **four rules**, all designed to be lightweight and flexible. First, the two habits:

Flocking, where the team comes together in a first meeting to initiate the work and together form the strategies, structures and systems they need to reach their goals.

Steering, monthly meetings with the goal to reflect on the work of the past month and set new goals. The outcome is an updated action plan and refreshed strategic plan.

With the habits in place, every team should steer toward four simple rules: Customer, alignment, autonomy and simplicity.

The first rule, your **customer** can be either external or internal, depending on the nature of the project or initiative. This direction is used to identify the real customer, understand their present and future needs, decide on a strategic direction and initiate the project.

The second rule, **alignment**, is there to improve communication and collaboration. Focus here is to identify internal misalignment, increase information exchange, find a common model for decision-making and make sure to have interpersonal rituals in place.

The third rule, **autonomy**, aims to empower risk-taking in an orderly manner. All through improving development across functions, the test-and-learn process as well as your rapid prototyping and also a responsive budget process.

The final rule, **simplicity**, is essential for reducing unnecessary complexity: Here focus is on recognizing complexity, approaching it in a new way, resisting increasing complexity as you scale and testing-and-learning to reduce it internally.

MEGATRENDS TECHNOLOGIES CASES FRAMEWORK EXECUTION TECHSTORM 44

BE SUSTAINABLE IN TIMES OF UNCERTAINTY

Corporate social responsibility, or CSR, is the act of running a business with an eye towards the social, environmental, and ethical impact the business's activities will have.[113] In the past, CSR focused on damage to the environment and ways in which a business could give back to its community. It was driven mostly by philanthropy – businesses gave money to support causes and to fuel clean up efforts when something went awry. Today, however, CSR has been expanded to include ethics, hiring processes, training, responsible purchasing, green solutions, and much more. As discussed earlier, no business exists in a vacuum, and while it is sometimes helpful to pretend that the contextual world surrounding it does not exist, a leader cannot afford to believe that the business does not impact on its context on multiple levels. Let us examine a business's CSR in terms of social, environmental, and ethical responsibilities with an eye towards how a business handles these responsibilities in uncertain times.

SOCIAL RESPONSIBILITY

A business' social responsibility has changed over the years. In fact, the debate over what exactly a business is responsible for has changed. No longer is it obligated simply to the shareholders, employees, and others it directly affects. Now, many consider a business to have a responsibility to society as a whole.[114]

This is because, again, a business affects more actors than those who directly interact with it. It impacts the entire context in which it operates. One company's actions can affect a community, a region, other businesses, and the entire industry of which it is a part. Today, leaders have to factor this into their decisions, and it all boils down to one single thought: create value for the business and the community as a whole.

Of course, this is easier said than done, and how one business goes about addressing its social responsibility is going to vary greatly from how other businesses do so. One thing, though, is not in question: businesses that shirk their social responsibility, in both times of crisis and stability, will be called out on it. Activist organizations, the government, the media, and other businesses do not hesitate to name and shame those that act irresponsibly.[115] CSR has become a way of life for businesses, and those that do not give it priority are doomed to face the consequences.

Few businesses make the news for making an ethical choice, even in times of uncertainty when others are not. Instead, it is those that are unethical that make headlines.

ENVIRONMENTAL RESPONSIBILITY

Becoming sustainable is no longer merely a selling point. It is now a strong driving influence on the free economy. Because of this, businesses that are not seen as environmentally friendly are taking a major business risk.[116] People no longer see the environment as something that is free for use. Instead, there is now a price on consuming natural resources, and as those resources become ever more scarce, that price will increase. In times of uncertainty, it is an easy fall back to start using natural resources that are easily available, but that comes at a price nowadays: a hit to the business' reputation. That is a hit that many simply cannot afford to take. The risk of losing a good percentage of customer base due to outrage over poor environmental stewardship is never worth the short-term benefits.

Being environmentally responsible often comes in two parts. The first is similar to the Hippocratic Oath taken by medical professionals: "First, do no harm." Businesses, even during times of uncertainty, should operate in such a way that they do not harm the environment. Of course, most people realize that this is a very, very difficult thing to do, and many resort to the next best thing: leaving as small a footprint on the world as possible.

The second part of being environmentally responsible is cleaning up any mess that a business may make. While most businesses work to make certain they do not end up in a PR nightmare like the one Exxon-Mobil went through when its ship spilled oil into the ocean, there is always that chance that something similar will happen. This is one area in which businesses must have a contingency plan in place. That, at the very least, shows a willingness to be environmentally responsible.

ETHICAL RESPONSIBILITY

While it's relatively easy to nail down the social and environmental responsibilities of a business and even measure them, it is somewhat more difficult to say what exactly a business' ethical responsibilities are. Generally, we view ethics as a photonegative: it is much easier to see when someone is not being ethical than it is to see when they are being ethical. Few businesses make the news for making an ethical choice, even in times of uncertainty when others are not. Instead, it is those that are unethical that make headlines.

Fortunately, many businesses are now creating and implementing ethical business standards, reporting habits, and transparency in their dealings.[117] Many large businesses are now voluntarily inviting external ethics organizations to examine their business practices and assist them in correcting any issues that are found.

While it may be the hardest to point out and to implement, being ethically responsible should be the first of the three CSR areas on which a business focuses. That's because when one is ethically responsible, being socially and environmentally responsible often requires little extra work.

TECHNOETHICS

The concept of technoethics is not as new as many people think. The term was coined in 1977 by Mario Bunge, a philosopher who saw the need to lay out principles and guidelines for the use of technology.[118] Today, this has become an interdisciplinary area that helps guide businesses, governments, and individuals in the ethical use of technology. One of the biggest areas of tech-

> While it may be the hardest to point out and to implement, being ethically responsible should be the first of the three CSR areas on which a business focuses.

noethics involves privacy. Where does an individual's right to privacy begin? If a person posts something to the internet via social media, is it instantly assumed to be public even if they allow restricted access to it? Do business leaders have the right to scour the internet for every little bit of dirt on a potential or current employee? Obviously, people do not want every detail of their lives put online, but it is much harder to see the line today when so many people voluntarily share this information.

Then there are questions pertaining to artificial intelligence, genetic manipulation, digital terrorism, and much more. In times of uncertainty, it is very easy to start committing what many would see as ethical violations via technology. In the US, this has already happened – the *Patriot Act* allowed the government to use technology to obtain information about individuals with little regard to their privacy, and the same debate is trending within the EU. Hackers do such things every day, some to steal sensitive information, others simply to see if they can. Even individuals may commit acts that are ethically questionable, such as downloading music illegally, or creating fake Facebook profiles in an attempt to gain access to information posted by ex partners.

Somewhere, lines must be drawn. Technoethics attempts to do this by examining how technology is used and where that use will take us. But it is more than simply discussing whether or not a technology should be used – that question is much too broad, and there are no

> Technology itself is a neutral concept; it is how that technology is used in specific situations, especially in uncertain times when the urge to abuse it is so strong, that we must question.

good answers. Instead, technoethics looks at more focused uses of technology. The overall idea is that technology itself is a neutral concept; it is how that technology is used in specific situations, especially in uncertain times when the urge to abuse it is so strong, that we must question.

ETHICS AND UNCERTAINTY

The conversation regarding CSR during times of stability is a much easier one to have than discussing ethics and responsibility during times of uncertainty. When a business is on the edge of failure, is it acceptable for that business to be less socially responsible in the sense that they may fund fewer community initiatives, scholarships, and so on? Is it acceptable for the business to opt to continue using manufacturing techniques that leave a carbon footprint when switching to a more expensive method would force the business into debt? These questions are why CSR continues to be an important factor in today's world.

However, there is no gray area when it comes to practising CSR. Leaders who fail to take ethical, environmental, and social factors into consideration while leading their businesses will face a severe backlash, sometimes to the extent that the business cannot recover.

CONCLUSION

Uncertain times place leaders in stressful situations. They may face challenges to their leadership, as can be seen in the fact that CEOs serve only about five years on average. They may find it difficult to implement innovative solutions and to even motivate their employees to be innovative. During these times, they may have to work to reorganize their business and, no matter what, they must always take social, ethical and environmental factors into consideration.

However, even though they may be dealing with uncertainty and chaos, strong leaders can successfully lead their businesses to stability and profitability without leaving ethics at the door. The most successful businesses in the world do this on a regular basis. After all, the only certainty in life is change, not failure.

SUSTAINABILITY TOOLBOX

The model on page 222 is used by one of Europe's largest private equity companies to assess potential investments as well as develop existing portfolio companies. The perspectives are both social impact in terms of human rights and ethics, and environmental impact in products, services and operations. Based on this, an investor or corporate management team can identify potential hazards in an investment case through mapping the level of social and environmental impact. Also, they can easily map a trajectory and create a corporate plan for development in these areas.

As with many models, the extremes (corners) of the model are the ones where the most potential impact can be seen going forward. Interesting also is that much of this progress can be achieved through the use of technology.

The "**do not invest**" corner is of course a very uncertain and complex area to invest. Often it is easy to just say no, but with the right due diligence, price level of the acquisition and management experience, this is a case where a sustainability-conscious investor can make the most impact.

The "**disruptive technologies**" corner is different in the sense that the understanding and awareness is high, but the company or industry lacks the necessary means and technologies to improve their environmental impact. Here, a good technological understanding is essential to make the case.

MEGATRENDS /// TECHNOLOGIES /// CASES /// FRAMEWORK /// **EXECUTION** /// TECHSTORM 44

The "**awareness and cultural change**" corner is the complete opposite. Here the environmental understanding is good, and there are also technical capabilities to handle the impact. From a social perspective, a lot has to be done, and here it is more of a challenge to change the mindset of the entire organization.

Being in the "**continuous improvement**" corner is of course somewhat of a luxury. Although this position is considered a potential entry barrier, the company can not sit back and relax. The entire business collective is moving in their direction and, as a leader in the field, it is important to stay ahead of the crowd.

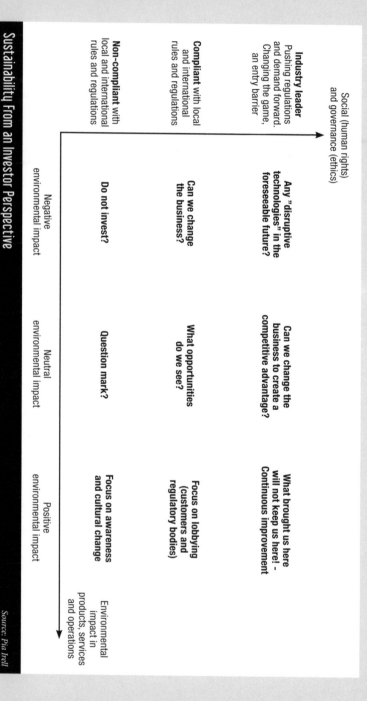

Sustainability From an Investor Perspective

Social (human rights)
and governance (ethics)

Industry leader
Pushing regulations
and demand forward.
Changing the game,
an entry barrier

Compliant with local
and international
rules and regulations

Non-compliant with
local and international
rules and regulations

Any "disruptive
technologies" in the
foreseeable future?

Can we change
the business?

Do not invest?

Can we change the
business to create a
competitive advantage?

What opportunities
do we see?

Question mark?

What brought us here
will not keep us here! –
Continuous improvement

Focus on lobbying
(customers and
regulatory bodies)

Focus on awareness
and cultural change

Negative
environmental impact

Neutral
environmental impact

Positive
environmental impact

Environmental
impact in
products, services
and operations

Source: Pia Irell

THE TECHSTORM
44 EMERGING
TECHNOLOGIES

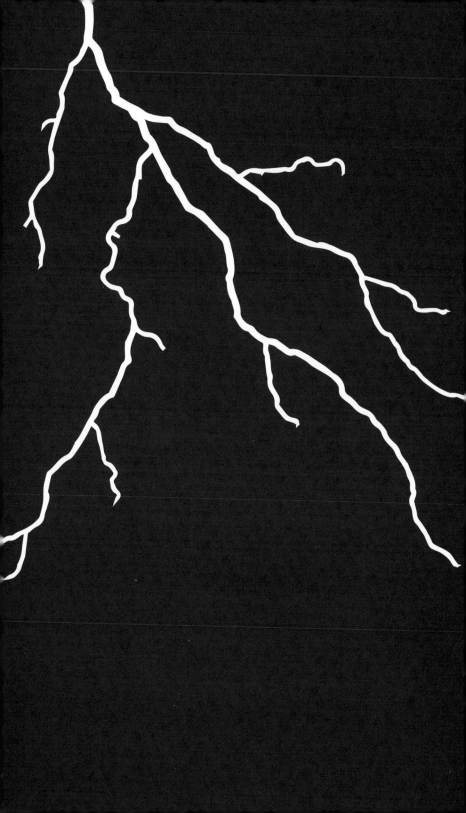

BITS

The field of **algorithms and machine learning** is focused on using advanced software to study pattern recognition. Programmers create algorithms that learn from given data and are capable of making predictions based on that information. Machine learning is useful in a number of fields, including programming, criminology, medical diagnosis, and financial analysis.

Artificial intelligence involves creating software that is capable of exhibiting intellectual thoughts and behaviors. Artificial intelligence has been defined as a system that is capable of understating its environments and working to maximize its own success. Artificial intelligence is one of the most divisive areas of technology today due to concerns over the ethics of creating intelligent machines.

Augmented reality (AR), is a way of augmenting or supplementing the physical environment by viewing it through a device such as a smartphone. The device augments the environment in real time and with semantic context. For example, an architect can view a site through a tablet and see the blueprints projected onto the work in progress.

Biochips are a type of miniaturized laboratory used in molecular biology. These chips can perform thousands of biochemical reactions simultaneously, providing researchers with a way of screening a large amount of data for disease diagnosis, poison detection, or countering bioterrorism. The biochip uses a microarray and transducer that sends signals to a processor, which generates the output.

Block chains are a type of distributed database that continuously expands to accommodate a growing amount of data. These data records are protected against revision and tampering, even by those with access to the data. The most common use of block chains keeping records of transactions made with cryptocurrencies such as Bitcoin, Dogecoin, and Ethereum.

Cloud computing uses remote servers to store, process, and manage data. This allows users to store information off site, providing a backup in the event of lost data. Remote servers also allow users to access their data from any location. These cloud servers are among the most secure and have a number of built in redundancies to ensure data is always available.

A **cryptocurrency** is a type of payment or exchange that uses cryptography to create a very secure transaction and to limit the amount of the currency created. They make use of a decentralized control system as opposed to most banking systems. Cryptocurrencies are often digital currencies or a type of alternative currency. The first and most famous cryptocurrency is Bitcoin.

Gamification is the method of applying elements generally found in games to other activities. These elements include things like scoring points, following specific rules, and engaging in competition with others. Gamification is often used as a way of increasing user engagement, learning, and productivity by offering users some kind of reward, even if that reward is a valueless achievement or meaningless points.

The **Internet of things** consists of all physical objects that are capable of connecting to the internet or other networks. While this does include computers, tablets, and smartphones, it also includes things like smart TVs, medical monitoring devices, pet microchips, smart thermostats, GPS, and any other device with network capability. Experts predict that by 2020, the internet of things will contain 50 billion devices.

Mobile payment technology allows vendors to take credit and debit card payments anywhere they can connect to a mobile phone network. Vendors either plug small mobile card readers into smartphones or tablets to swipe cards, or use near field communication (NFC) wireless connections to perform transactions. Well known mobile payment systems include Square, PayPal, and Apple Pay.

A **natural interface** is any user interface that is controlled by the user's voice, gestures, or even gaze. This type of interface is much less conspicuous because it involves no use of artificial input devices such as a keyboard, mouse, or so on. Examples of natural interfaces include Apple's Siri, reacting to voice commands, and the Xbox Kinect, a device controlled by performing gestures in front of a camera.

Novel computing is an umbrella term for any new, innovative type of computing. Many technologies begin under the novel-computing category before becoming standard. These technologies cover a wide range of industries, and many focus on taking concepts previously considered science fiction and making them a reality. Current novel computing areas include bio-computing, nanotechnology, wearable technology, and optical computing.

Online education consists of students and professors meeting in a virtual classroom setting. Using chat, multimedia, whiteboards, and video teleconferencing, students from many different locations come together with the professor in an online setting rather than attending class in a physical classroom. Online education has been used for all grade levels, and some universities offer degree programs that are taught entirely, or mostly, online.

The discipline of **quantum computing** looks at how computer systems can use quantum mechanics to operate. It applies theories such as entanglement and superposition to create computers that are not limited by today's systems. This would allow them to process data at a much higher rate, for example to be used in cryptology. To date, a limited number of quantum operations have been executed, but a true quantum computer has (probably) not been built.

Smart dust makes use of microelectromechanical systems composed of robots, sensors, or other devices that can detect vibration, light, temperature, chemicals, or magnetism. These devices are controlled wirelessly and are often distributed across the target area to perform a variety of tasks. Smart dust must have a powerful controller antenna because the actual devices are too small to maintain communication over long distances.

Speech-to-speech translation makes use of a computer program to translate what one person is saying into another language and to recite the translation to another person. It is often used for long distance conversations when no human translator is available at one end or both. Due to difficulty translating some idioms and phrases, however, these programs often offer a literal translation instead of a more accurate transliteration.

A **terabit optical network** is a next generation computer network that will be faster and more secure than current networks. These optical networks will be a multi-service platform capable of supporting commercial, residential, mobile, and special applications. Due to current bandwidth needs and their anticipated increases, any next generation network will most likely require speeds of at least terabit level.

Virtual reality technology simulates an environment in three dimensions around a person. Current virtual reality involves the user wearing a special set of 3D goggles to view the environment and special gloves to interact with it. While early attempts at virtual reality were fairly crude, today, technology has improved to the point that very realistic simulations can be created.

Wearables, or wearable technology, is a category of technology that includes any device that has been micronized to the point that it can be worn on the human body comfortably and (almost) without notice. This includes workout and medical monitoring, communications, and computing devices. Two early examples of wearables include Google Glass and the Apple watch.

The concept of **widespread global internet** access is about creating a world in which all individuals have access to the internet, regardless of where they live or their individual resources. It would allow for greater worldwide collaboration, bring education to those who do not have these opportunities, and allow businesses to market to a truly global audience.

ATOMS

3D scanning and printing allows an object to be scanned into a computer, then recreated using a 3D printer. This technology makes it easy to replicate items without the need of more expensive manufacturing equipment. 3D scanning can also be used to digitize any object, while 3D printing can be used to create a wide variety of shapes, components, and products, some of which cannot be manufactured using other techniques.

Advanced materials are materials that have been created to help advance technology. These materials are designed at atomic level by materials scientists who design each one for a specific purpose. An advanced type of metal, for example, may be designed for incredible durability, while an advanced type of plastic may be designed with improved flexibility.

Autonomous or self-driving vehicles use computers, sensors, GPS devices, and maps to transport people or items safely from one point to another without the need for a driver. The exterior is lined with sensors that detect objects and automatically stop the car before a collision. Several autonomous vehicle projects are undergoing testing with impressive results and the technology is advancing quickly.

A **drone** is a remote controlled vehicle, generally an air vehicle, that has long-range capabilities.

Drones may be autonomous and controlled via computer or may be piloted by an operator. Drones have a number of uses, including surveillance, delivery of materials, and military capabilities. Short-range drones are available to the general public, while long-range drones are in use by the military.

High power storage systems are a critical component of advanced energy storage systems. They have the capability to store a high rate of energy very quickly from a variety of sources, including renewable sources. They also discharge power quickly and can supply energy within a second. These storage cells do not lose energy as quickly, allowing for long-term storage of power. As a result, these systems are ideal for emergency backup systems.

Nanobots are microscopic programmable robots that can be used in a variety of different ways. These robots can interact with objects on a nanoscopic level, entering molecules, human cells, and technology. Potential uses include using nanobots to destroy cancerous cells, detect chemical spills, and repair microchips. Nanobots capable of replication may be used to build entire pieces of equipment with the correct programming.

The field of **new energy solutions** looks at ways of reducing or eliminating our dependency on fossil fuels while making energy production, storage and use more efficient. Some areas of this field look at using renewable resources such as solar, wind, and hydro power, while others focus on designing new fuel cells and engines that require less energy to operate.

Smart robots are robots that make use of evolving and learning algorithms in order to improvise. These robots are designed to learn how to use objects around them to complete various tasks. They do not have to be programmed to use specific objects for specific functions, but instead build a program themselves based on trial and error with objects with which they interact or have previously encountered.

NEURONS

A **brain transplant**, sometimes referred to as a whole body transplant, is the process of removing the brain from one body and transplanting it into the body of another organism. Only the brain is transferred, not the entire head. This technology is in its infancy, and a successful brain transplant has yet to be completed.

Brain or mind uploading involves uploading an individual's entire personality, memory, and attributes to a computer network or other type of artificial containment system. This hypothetical process would effectively allow humans to live forever by uploading their brains to computer networks, robotic bodies, or even cloned biological bodies. It may also be possible to create complete clones using a copy and transfer method of uploading.

A **brain-computer interface** is an interface that directly connects the brain to a computer device. Research into these interfaces has been done since the 1970s, leading to breakthroughs in the areas of vision, prosthesis, and motor control. Brain-computer interfaces can allow those with a disability to regain all or partial functionality, plus they may be capable of enhancing human capabilities.

Neurobusiness is taking the concepts and theories of neuro-science and applying them in a business context. This is done to gain insight into customer needs and satisfaction. Much of this insight is based on analyzing why people do things instinctively and learning how to use these reactions in marketing, decision-making, and other business related areas.

Neurotechnology is any type of technology that allows us to understand how the brain functions. It includes looking at higher brain activity, thought and consciousness. This technology can be used to improve brain function in a number of ways, including regulating brain activity and stimulating areas that are no longer active, for example the treatment of Parkinson's disease.

GENES

3D bioprinting takes the concepts and techniques used in 3D printing and applies them to living cells. It allows for the creation of spatially controlled cell patterns that function like natural cells. This technology is capable of printing tissues that could be used for reconstructive surgery and, in the future, may even be capable of creating organs for transplant patients.

Biometrics is the use of biological characteristics such as a fingerprint, voice, retina pattern, facial structure, vein pattern, or other type of characteristic to authenticate the user. These biometrics are unique to the user and cannot easily be copied, which means biometric security is much stronger than relying on a username and password combination.

Genetic characterization is the process of taking various genetic sequences and comparing them against one another. It has been used in public health to identify viruses and track their evolution. By lowering the cost so that genetic characterization can be performed on individuals on a regular basis, it will be possible to track mutations and may lead to a solution for genetic illnesses.

Cloning is the act of taking the DNA from one plant or animal and duplicating it. In this manner, everything from a single cell to an entire living organism can be cloned. Cloning a live animal was successfully done in 1996 when Dolly the Sheep was created from adult somatic cells. Cloning has a number of potential medical uses, including creating cloned organs for transplant patients.

e-health is the combination of healthcare and electric communications, processing, and record keeping. The exact definition of e-health is varied, with many organizations having their own unique idea of what it entails. Generally, it involves any use of technology in the healthcare industry and may include anything from electronic health records to cyber-medicine and self-monitoring apps and other devices.

Genetic modification is the act of manipulating an organism's genome to change the makeup of that organism's cells. It often involves inserting, removing, or replacing DNA via artificially engineered nucleases such as clustered regularly interspaced short palindromic repeats (CRISPR). CRISPRs have been used in immunization, disease research, agriculture, and may be invaluable in the treatment of illnesses such as cystic fibrosis.

A **genetically modified organism (GMO)** is an organism that has had its genetic material altered in some way. Creating GMOs involves inserting, deleting, or changing the genes of the organism and may include adding genes from a different organism into another's DNA. GMOs are most commonly associated with modified plants and crops, although genetically modified animals have been created.

Human augmentation or enhancement is the attempt, either temporarily or permanently, to change the human body naturally or artificially. This includes modifications that both improve upon existing human capacities and create new capacities that are currently beyond humanity. Cosmetic enhancement, prosthetics, medical implants, neurostimulation, and even using technology that makes life more efficient can be considered forms of human augmentation.

The term **longevity** is often defined as life expectancy, but it is also often used in discussions on extending human life. Work in the area of longevity extends across a number of disciplines and looks at ways of eliminating disease, slowing down ageing, and repairing or regenerating damage to the human body.

The concept of **quantified self** is the concept of breaking a person's daily life down into sets of data using technology. This allows a person to see exactly what they have consumed, their moods, their performance levels, and even things such as the quality of the air they have been breathing. It may also be referred to as life logging, and it often makes use of a number of wearable technologies.

EXECUTE IN TIMES OF UNCERTAINTY

MEGATRENDS

TECHNOLOGIES

CASES

FRAMEWORK

EXECUTION

TECHSTORM 44

Synthetic biology is a specialization that involves biology, computer engineering, biophysics, and genetics. It focuses on designing and creating artificial versions of biological systems or using technology to repair damaged organisms via created organs, blood, and other natural substances. Examples of synthetic biology include sequencing DNA, synthesizing genomes, and designing proteins.

ENDNOTES

1. Center for Health Workforce Studies School of Public Health. *The Impact of the Aging Population on the Health Workforce in the United States: Summary of Key Findings.,* University at Albany; 2006.

2. Watson, Richard. *Future Files: A Brief History of the Next 50 Years.* Nicholas Brealey Publishing; 2009.

3. AHRQ. *Medical Expenditure Survey Panel*; 2014. http://meps.ahrq.gov/mepsweb/data_files/publications/st429/ stat429.pdf

4. OECD Indicators. *Health at a Glance*; 2013, p155.

5. Cornish, Edward *Futuring: The Exploration of the Future.* World Future Society; 2005.

6. Smith, Laurence. *The World in 2050: Four Forces Shaping Civilization's Northern Future.* Dutton Adult; 2010.

7. Burrows, Matthew. *The Future, Declassified: Mega-trends That Will Undo the World Unless We Take Action.* Palgrave Macmillan Trade; 2014.

8. KPMG. *What Are Global Megatrends?*; 2013 http://www.kpmg.com/global/en/issuesandinsights/ articlespublications/future-state-government/pages/what-are-the- global-megatrends.aspx

9. *Megatrends 2015.* EY; 2015 http://www.ey.com/Publication/vwLUAssets/ey-megatrends- report-2015/$FILE/ey-megatrends-report-2015.pdf

10. Smith, Laurence. *The World in 2050: Four Forces Shaping Civilization's Northern Future.* Dutton Adult; 2010.

11. Al Gore,. *The Future*. Virgin Digital; 2013

12. US Environmental Protection Agency. *Climate Change Science Overview*; 2014.

13. *Megatrends* 2015. EY; 2015.
    http://www.ey.com/Publication/vwLUAssets/ey-megatrends-report-2015/$FILE/ey-megatrends-report-2015.pdf

14. *Megatrends 2015.* EY; 2015.
    http://www.ey.com/Publication/vwLUAssets/ey-megatrends-report-2015/$FILE/ey-megatrends-report-2015.pdf

15. United Nations, Department of Economic and Social Affairs. *World Population Prospects, the 2015 Revision*; 2015.
    http://esa.un.org/unpd/wpp/Graphs/

16. United Nations, Department of Economic and Social Affairs. *World's population increasingly urban with more than half living in urban areas*; 2015.
    https://www.un.org/development/desa/en/news/population/world-urbanization-prospects.html

17. Cornish, Edward. *Futuring: The Exploration of the Future.* World Future Society; 2005.

18. Cornish, Edward. 2005. *Futuring: The Exploration of the Future.* World Future Society; 2005.

19. Watson, Richard. *Future Files: A Brief History of the Next 50 Years.* Nicholas Brealey Publishing; 2009.

20. Caprino, Kathy. *6 Ways Pushing Past Your Comfort Zone Is Critical To Success.* Forbes; 2014.

21. KPMG. *What Are Global Megatrends?* 2013
    http://www.kpmg.com/global/en/issuesandinsights/articlespublications/future-state-government/pages/what-are-the-global-megatrends.aspx

22. Burrows, Matthew. *The Future, Declassified: Mega-trends That Will Undo the World Unless We Take Action*. Palgrave Macmillan Trade; 2014.

23. Watson, Richard. *Future Files: A Brief History of the Next 50 Years*. Nicholas Brealey Publishing; 2009

24. Globalization 101. *What is Globalization?*; 2015 http://www.globalization101.org/what-is-globalization/

25. Cornish, Edward. *Futuring: The Exploration of the Future*. World Future Society; 2005.

26. Al Gore,. *The Future*. Virgin Digital; 2013.

27. Smith, Laurence. *The World in 2050: Four Forces Shaping Civilization's Northern Future*. Dutton Adult; 2010.

28. *Megatrends 2015*. EY; 2015 http://www.ey.com/Publication/vwLUAssets/ey-megatrends-report-2015/$FILE/ey-megatrends-report-2015.pdf

29. *Megatrends 2015*. EY; 2015 http://www.ey.com/Publication/vwLUAssets/ey-megatrends-report-2015/$FILE/ey-megatrends-report-2015.pdf

30. Technology waves, or Kondratiev waves, are named after Soviet economist Nikolai Kondratieff, who originally defined these cycles in his 1925 book *The Major Economic Cycles*.

31. Lipsey, Richard G, Carlaw, Kenneth I, Bekar, Clifford T; Economic *Transformations - General Purpose Technologies and Long Term Economic Growth*. Oxford University Press; 2005.

32. Schumpeter, Joseph A; *Business Cycles: A Theoretical, Historical and Statistical Analysis of the Capitalist Process*. McGraw-Hill; 1939.

33. Fogel, Robert W. *The Escape from Hunger and Premature Death, 1700–2100*. London: Cambridge University Press; 2004.

34. Timberlake, Jr, Richard H. Panic of 1837. In: Glasner, David; Cooley, Thomas F, eds. *Business cycles and depressions: an encyclopedia*. New York: Garland Publishing; 1997.

35. Freeman, Chris, Soete Luc. *The Economics of Industrial Innovation*. The MIT Press; 1997.

36. Schumpeter, Joseph A. *Business Cycles: A Theoretical, Historical and Statistical Analysis of the Capitalist Process*. McGraw-Hill; 1939.

37. Musson, AE. The Great Depression in Britain, 1873-1896: "A Reappraisal". *The Journal of Economic History*. Cambridge University Press; 1959.

38. By comparison, GDP fell less than 1% from 2008 to 2009 in the Great Recession. Lowenstein, Roger. History Repeating. *Wall Street Journal Jan 14*; 2015

39. Perez, Carlota. *Technological revolutions and techno-economic paradigms*. Working Papers in Technology Governance and Economic Dynamics. The Other Canon Foundation, Norway and Tallinn University of Technology, Tallinn; January 20, 2009

40. Kondratiev waves, named after Soviet economist Nikolai Kondratiev (1892-1938). Also called supercycles, great surges, long waves, K-waves or the long economic cycle.

41. National Heart, Lung, and Blood Institute, http://grants.nih.gov/grants/guide/notice-files/NOT- HL-03-005.html

42. National Nanotechnology Initiative, 2000

43. Smart Insights. *Mobile Marketing Statistics 2015*. http://www.smartinsights.com/mobile-marketing/mobile-marketing-analytics/mobile-marketing-statistics/

44. Turing, Alan M. Computing Machinery and Intelligence. MIND - *Quarterly Review of Psychology and Philosophy*; October 1950.

45. Wired Magazine. *IBMs Watson is better at diagnosing cancer than human doctors*; February 2013.
http://www.wired.co.uk/news/archive/2013-02/11/ibm-watson-medical-doctor

46. Sciencelearn.org
http://www.sciencelearn.org.nz/Contexts/Nanoscience/NZ-Research/Nanoscience

47. Wired.com; 2013
http://www.wired.com/wiredscience/2013/02/three-awesome-tools-scientists-may-use-to-map-your-brain-in-the-future/

48. Nguyen, Peter, Botyanszki, Zsofia et al. Programmable biofilm-based materials from engineered curli nano-fibres. *Nature Communications* 5: 4945; Sept 17, 2014. doi:10.1038/ncomms5945. PMID 25229329.

49. The Global Technology Revolution, RAND; 2001.

50. Gleick, James; Faster – *The Acceleration of Just About Everything*. Vintage Books; 1999.

51. *The Man Who Invented Management*, Bloomberg Business Week; November 27, 2005.
http://www.bloomberg.com/bw/stories/2005-11-27/the-man-who-invented-management.

52. Davenport Thomas H, Prusak Laurence. *Working Knowledge - How Organizations Manage What They Know*. Harvard Business School Press; 2000; 53

53. Venter, J Craig et al. *The Sequence of the Human Genome*. Science; 16 February 2001.

54. https://en.wikipedia.org/wiki/Celera_Corporation

55. National Human Genome Research Institute.
http://www.genome.gov/sequencingcosts/

56. https://press.spotify.com/se/information/

57. Calculation based on 20 million subscribers paying US$10 per month.

58. *Spotify Value tops $8 Billion as Investors Bet on Streaming.* Bloomberg; 2015 www.bloomberg.com/news/articles/2015-06-10/spotify-valued-at-8-2-billion-as-teliasonera-buys-stake

59. Day, George S; Schoemaker, Paul J H: Avoiding the Pitfalls of Emerging Technologies. *California Management Review.* Vol. 42 (2); Winter 2000, 8-33.

60. http://www.kodak.com/ek/US/en/Kodak_Completes_527_Million_Transaction_Related_to_Digital_Imaging_Patents.htm

61. Pisano, Gary P: You Need an Innovation Strategy. *Harvard Business Review*; June 2015

62. Day, George S, Schoemaker, Paul J H: Avoiding the Pitfalls of Emerging Technologies. *California Management Review.* Vol. 42 (2); Winter 2000, 8-33.

63. Day, George S. Schoemaker, Paul J H: Avoiding the Pitfalls of Emerging Technologies. *California Management Review.* Vol. 42 (2); Winter 2000, 8-33.

64. Johnson, Mark W, Christensen, Clayton M, Kagermann, Henning. *Reinventing Your Business Model. The Strategy Process - Concepts, Contexts, Cases.* Pearson, Harlow; 2014.

65. Ford, Henry; Crowther, Samuel. *My Life and Work.* New York, US: Garden City Publishing Company, Inc; 1922. Various republications, including ISBN 9781406500189. Original is public domain in US. Also available at Google Books.

66. Ford, Henry; Crowther, Samuel. *Today and Tomorrow.* Garden City, New York, USA: Doubleday, Page & Company. Co-edition, 1926, London, William Heinemann. Various republications, including ISBN 0-915299-36-4.

67. Sloan, Alfred P. McDonald, John, ed, *My Years with General Motors*, Garden City, NY, US: Doubleday; 1964, LCCN 64011306, OCLC 802024. Republished in 1990 with a new introduction by Peter Drucker (ISBN 978-0385042352).

68. Imai, Masaaki. *Kaizen: The Key to Japan's Competitive Success*. New York: Random House; 1986.

69. Drucker, Peter F. *The Practice of Management*. New York: Harper & Brothers; 1954.

70. Kotler, Philip. *Marketing Management: Analysis, Planning and Control*. Englewood Cliffs, NJ. Prentice-Hall; 1967.

71. Porter, ME. *Competitive Strategy*. Free Press, New York; 1980.

72. Porter, ME. *Competitive Advantage*. Free Press, New York; 1985

73. Boyd, John R. *Destruction and Creation* (PDF). US Army Command and General Staff College; September 3, 1976.

74. Ries, Eric. *The Lean Startup*

75. Revans, Reginald. *Action learning: New techniques for management*. London: Blond & Briggs, Ltd; 1980.

76. Richard Mignogna. http://richmignogna.blogspot.se

77. http://www.gartner.com/technology/research/methodologies/hype-cycle.jsp

78. Moore, Geoffrey M. *Crossing the Chasm*.

79. Johnson, Mark W, Christensen, Clayton M, Kagermann, Henning. *Reinventing Your Business Model. The Strategy Process - Concepts, Contexts, Cases*. Pearson. Harlow; 2014.

80. Johnson, Mark W, Christensen, Clayton M, Kagermann, Henning. *Reinventing Your Business Model. The Strategy Process - Concepts, Contexts, Cases*. Pearson, Harlow; 2014.

81. Wikipedia: time management. https://en.wikipedia.org/wiki/Time_management

82. Adapted from Courtney, Kirkland, and Viguerie. Strategy Un
   Uncertainty. *Harvard Business Review*; November-December 1

83. Wikipedia: VUCA.
   https://en.wikipedia.org/wiki/Volatility,_uncertainty,_complexity_
   and_ambiguity

84. Bennett, Nathan G, Lemoine, James. What VUCA Really Means
   for You. *Harvard Business Review*; January-February 2014.

85. Courtney, Kirkland, and Viguerie. Strategy Under Uncertainty.
   Harvard Business Review; November-December 1997.

86. Courtney, Kirkland, and Viguerie. Strategy Under Uncertainty.
   Harvard Business Review; November-December 1997.

87. Courtney, Kirkland, and Viguerie. Strategy Under Uncertainty.
   Harvard Business Review; November-December 1997.

88. Courtney, Kirkland, and Viguerie. Strategy Under Uncertainty.
   Harvard Business Review; November-December 1997.

89. *Surviving Disruption*,p58. Wessel, Maxwell; Christensen,
   Clayton M. Surviving Disruption. Harvard Business Review,
   December 2012

90. Wessel, Maxwell; Christensen, Clayton M. Surviving Disruption.
   Harvard Business Review, December 2012

91. *Routes to Resilience*, p71. Gilbert, Clark; Eyring Matthew; Foster,
   Richard N. Two Routes to Resilience. Harvard Business Review,
   December 2012

92. Courtney, Kirkland, and Viguerie. Strategy Under Uncertainty.
   Harvard Business Review; November-December 1997.

92. Carnegie Council for Ethics in International Affairs. Global
   Ethics Forum: *A Conversation with Douglas Rushkoff, Digital
   Media Expert;* 2014 [updated 2014 April 24; cited 2015 June
   10]. Available from http://www.carnegiecouncil.org/studio/
   multimedia/20140424b/index.html

...amic Management: Better Decisions in Uncertain
...y & Company; 2009 [updated 2009 December;
...ne 10]. Available from http://www.mckinsey.com/
...anaging_in_uncertainty/dynamic_management_better_
...ns_in_uncertain_times

...emmer, Ian. *How to Lead in Ambiguous Times.*
Strategy+Business; 2015 [updated 2015 February 2; cited 2015
June 10]. Available from http://www.strategy-business.com/
article/00306?gko=1c731

95. Hildebrand, Carol. *Lessons in Transformation From the Digital
     Masters.* Forbes; 2014 [2014 October 3; cited 2015 June 10].
     Available from http://www.forbes.com/sites/oracle/2014/10/03/
     lessons-in-transformation-from-the-digital-masters/

96. Dale Carnegie Training. Employee Engagement During Times of
     Uncertainty. Dale Carnegie Training; 2015 [nd; cited 2015 Juen
     10]. Available from http://atlanta.dalecarnegie.com/employee_
     engagement_during_times_of_uncertainty/

97. Amerland, David. *5 Ways to Inspire Innovation (And Plan for
     Disruption.* Forbes; 2014 [2014 July 14; cited 2015 June 10].
     Available from http://www.forbes.com/sites/netapp/2014/07/14/
     innovation-and-disruption/

98. Forbes. *Lessons In Transformation From The Digital Masters*;
     October 3, 2014.
     http://www.forbes.com/sites/oracle/2014/10/03/lessons-in-
     transformation-from-the-digital-masters/

99. Daum, Kevin. *How Smart Leaders Manage Uncertain Times*; 2013
     [2013 October 9; cited 2015 June 10]. Available from
     http://www.inc.com/kevin-daum/how-to-make-the-most-of-
     uncertain-times.html

100. Mui, Chunka. *8 Make-or-Break Rules for Corporate Innovation.*
     Forbes; 2014 [2014 July 22; cited 2015 June 10]. Available from
     http://www.forbes.com/sites/chunkamui/2014/07/22/8-make-or-
     break-rules-for-corporate-innovation/

101. de Jong M, Marston N, Roth E. *The Eight Essential of Innovation*. McKinsey Quarterly; 2015 [2015 April; cited 2015 June 10]. Available from http://www.mckinsey.com/insights/innovation/the_eight_essentials_of_innovation

102. Neilson GL, Estupinan J, Sethi B. *10 Principles of Organization Design*. Strategy+Business; 2015 [2015 March 23; cited 2015 June 20]. Available from http://www.strategy-business.com/article/00318?gko=c7329

103. Garza, Joseph A. *The Rise of Thought Leadership: Visionaries, Innovators, Problem Solvers*. National Networkers Association. 2015 [2015 January 20; cited 2015 June 10]. Available from https://nationalnetwork.wordpress.com/2015/01/20/the-rise-of-thought-leadership-visionaries-innovators-problem-solvers/

104. Hagel J, Brown JS, Davison L. Are All Employees Knowledge Workers? *Harvard Business Review*; 2010 [2010 April 5; cited 2015 June 10]. Available from https://hbr.org/2010/04/are-all-employees-knowledge-wo.html

105. Adrian, Anne. *Skills for the Future Knowledge Worker. National Association of Extension Program and Staff Development Professionals*. Slideshare; 2013 [2013 De-cember; cited 2015 June 10]. Available from http://www.slideshare.net/aafromaa/prof-devsession

106. Neilson GL, Estupinan J, Sethi B. *10 Principles of Organization Design*. Strategy+Business. 2015 [2015 March 23; cited 2015 June 20]. Available from http://www.strategy-business.com/article/00318?gko=c7329

107. McLaughlin K, McMillion D. *Business and Society in the Coming Decades*. McKinsey & Company; 2015 [2015 April; cited 2015 June 10]. Available from http://www.mckinsey.com/insights/strategy/business_and_society_in_the_coming_decades

108. Porter ME, Kramer MR. Strategy and Society: The Link Between Competitive Advantage and Corporate Social Responsibility. *Harvard Business Review*; 2006 [2006 December; cited 2015 June 10]. Available from https://hbr.org/2006/12/strategy-and-society-the-link-between-competitive-advantage-and-corporate-social-responsibility

109. Garza, Joseph A. *The Rise of Thought Leadership: Visionaries, Innovators, Problem Solvers.* National Networkers Association. 2015 [2015 January 20; cited 2015 June 10]. Available from https://nationalnetwork.wordpress.com/2015/01/20/the-rise-of-thought-leadership-visionaries-innovators-problem-solvers/

110. Hagel J, Brown JS, Davison L. *Are All Employees Knowledge Workers?* Harvard Business Review. 2010 [2010 April 5; cited 2015 June 10]. Available from https://hbr.org/2010/04/are-all-employees-knowledge-wo.html

111. Adrian, Anne. *Skills for the Future Knowledge Worker.* National Association of Extension Program and Staff Development Professionals. Slideshare. 2013 [2013 December; cited 2015 June 10]. Available from http://www.slideshare.net/aafromaa/prof-devsession

112. Neilson GL, Estupinan J, Sethi B. *10 Principles of Organization Design.* Strategy+Business. 2015 [2015 March 23; cited 2015 June 20]. Available from http://www.strategy-business.com/article/00318?gko=c7329

113. As You Sow. *Corporate Social Responsibility.* As You Sow. [nd; cited 2015 June 10]. Available from http://www.asyousow.org/about-us/theory-of-change/corporate-social-responsibility/

114. McLaughlin K, McMillion D. *Business and Society in the Coming Decades.* McKinsey & Company. 2015 [2015 April; cited 2015 June 10]. Available from http://www.mckinsey.com/insights/strategy/business_and_society_in_the_coming_decades

115. Porter ME, Kramer MR. *Strategy and Society: The Link Between Competitive Advantage and Corporate Social Responsibility.* Harvard Business Review. 2006 [2006 December; cited 2015 June 10]. Available from https://hbr.org/2006/12/strategy-and-society-the-link-between-competitive-advantage-and-corporate-social-responsibility

116. Allianz Global Investors. *The "Green" Kondratieff – or Why Crises Can be a Good Thing.* Allianz Global Investors. 2013 [March 2013; cited 2015 June 10]. Available from https://www.allianzglobalinvestors.de/MDBWS/doc/BR_AnalysenTrends_Gruener-Kondratieff_EN_EN_032013.pdf?b109d132aaca3fa2cec9ae8b342b956d31836dfe

117. Jacobs, Kristina. *The Ethics of Corporate Social Responsibility.* International Center for Ethics, Justice, and Public Life. 2013 [2013 November; cited 2015 June 10]. Available from http://www.brandeis.edu/ethics/ethicalinquiry/2013/November.html

118. https://en.wikipedia.org/wiki/Technoethics

FURTHER READING

Arthur, Brian W. *Increasing Returns and Path Dependence in the Economy.* The University of Michigan Press; 1994.

Arthur, Brian W. *The Nature of Technology - What it is and How it Evolves.* Free Press; 2009.

Atkinson, Anthony B, Stiglitz, Joseph E. Lectures on public economics. McGraw-Hill; 1980.

Belfiore, Michael. *The Department of Mad Scientists.* Smithsonian Books; 2009.

Bell, Wendell. *Foundations of Futures Studies - History, Purposes and Knowledge.* Transaction Publishers; 2011.

Benyus, Janine M. *Biomimicry - Innovation Inspired by Nature.* Harper Perennial; 1997.

Berleant, Daniel. *The Human Race to the Future - What Could Happen and What To Do.* Lifeboat Foundation; 2013.

Bradfield Moody, James, Nogrady, Bianca. *The Sixth Wave - How to Succeed in a Resource limited World.* Vintage Books; 2010.

Brockman, John (Ed). *The Next Fifty Years - Science in the First Half of the Twenty-First Century.* Vintage Books; 2002.

Brockman, John (Ed). *Is the Internet Changing the Way You Think?* Harper Perennial; 2011.

Broderick, Damien. *The Spike - How Our Lives are Being Transformed by Rapidly Advancing Technologies.* Tom Doherty Associates; 2001.

Broderick, Damien (Ed). *Year Million - Science at the Far Edge of Knowledge.* Atlas & Co; 2008.

Brynjolfsson, Erik, McAfee, Andrew. *Race Against the Machine.* Digital Frontier Press; 2011.

Buchanan, Allen. *Beyond Humanity.* Oxford University Press; 2011.

Buckingham, Jane, Ward, Tiffany. *What's Next - The Experts' Guide.* HarperCollins; 2008.

Canton, James. The Extreme Futures. Penguin Books; 2006.

Castells, Manuel. *The Information Age. Economy, Society and Culture. Volume I: The Rise of the Network Society.* Blackwell Publishers; 1996.

Castells, Manuel. *The Information Age. Economy, Society and Culture. Volume II: The Power of Identity.* Blackwell Publishers; 1997.

Castells, Manuel. *The Information Age. Economy, Society and Culture. Volume III: End of the Millennium.* Blackwell Publishers; 2000.

Casti, John; *X-events – The Collapse of Everything.* Harper Collins; 2012.

Chandler, Alfred Dupont. *Strategy and Structure – Chapters in the History of the Industrial Enterprise.* MIT Press; 1962.

Chesley, Harry. *Nanotechnology.* MIT Press; 1996.

Christensen, Clayton M. *The Innovator's Dilemma.* Harper Business; 2000.

Church, George, Regis (Ed). *Regenesis - How Synthetic Biology Will Reinvent Nature and Ourselves.* Perseus Books; 2012.

Cornish, Edward. *Futuring – The Exploration of the Future.* The World Future Society; 2004.

David, Paul A. *Technical Choice Innovation and Economic Growth.* Cambridge University Press; 1975.

David, Paul A, Hall, H Bronwhyn, Toll, Andrew A, *Is public R&D a complement or a substitute for private R&D*. NBER; 1999.

Davenport and Prusak. *How organizations manage what they know.* Harvard Business School; 2000.

de Grey, Aubrey, Rae, Michael. *Ending Aging - The Rejuvenation Breakthroughs That Could Reverse Human Aging in Our Lifetime.* St Martin's Press; 2007.

Diamandis, Peter H, Kotler Steven. *Abundance - The Future is Better than You Think.* Simon & Schuster; 2012.

Dosi Giovanni (ed.). *Technical Change and Economic Theory.* Pinter Publishers; 1988.

Drexler, K Eric. *Radical Abundance - How a Revolution in Nanotechnology Will Change Civilization.* Public Affairs; 2013.

Fahey, Liam, Randall, Robert M. *Learning From the Future – Competitive Foresight Scenarios.* John Wiley & Sons; 1998.

Fara, Patricia. *Science - A Four Thousand Year History.* Oxford University Press; 2009.

Fenn, Jackie, Raskino, Mark. *Mastering the Hype Cycle - How to Choose the Right Innovation at the Right Time.* Harvard Business Press; 2008.

Ferguson, Marilyn. *The Aquarian Conspiracy in our time.* St Martins Press; 1976.

Flatow, Ira. *Present at the Future.* HarperCollins; 2007.

Florida, Richard. *The Rise of the Creative Class.* Basic Books; 2002.

Ford, Martin. *The Lights in the Tunnel - Automation, Accelerating Technology and the Economy of the Future.* Acculant; 2009.

Freeman, Chris, Soete Luc. *The Economics of Industrial Innovation.* The MIT Press; 1997.

Frenay, Robert. *Pulse - The Coming Age of Systems and Machines Inspired by Living Things.* The University of Nebraska Press; 2008.

Friedman, George. *The Next 100 Years - A Forecast For the 21st Century.* Anchor Books; 2009.

Gee, Henry (Ed). *Futures From Nature - 100 Speculative Fictions.* Macmillan Publishers; 2007.

Gladwell, Malcolm. *The Tipping Point – How Little Things Can Make a Big Difference.* Abacus; 2001.

Gleick, James. *Faster – The Acceleration of Just About Everything.* Vintage Books; 1999.

Gleick, James. *What Just Happened - A Chronicle From the Information Frontier.* Vintage Books; 2002.

Gleick, James. *The Information - A History, A Theory, A Flood.* Pantheon Books; 2011.

Gordon, Adam. *Future Savvy.* Amacom; 2009.

Harmon, Fred. *Business 2010 – Five Forces That Will Reshape Business.* Kiplinger Books; 2001.

Hogue, John. *Nostradamus - The Complete Prophecies.* Element; 1997.

Kaku, Michio. *Visions - How Science Will Revolutionize the 21st Century and Beyond.* Oxford University Press; 1998.

Kaku, Michio. *Physics of the Future.* Doubleday; 2011.

Kelly, Kevin. *What Technology Wants.* Viking Books; 2010.

Kojm, Christopher (Ed). *Global Trends 2030 - Alternate Worlds.* National Intelligence Council; 2012.

Kristensson-Uggla, Bengt; *Gränspassager - Bildning i tolkningens tid.* Santerus Förlag; 2012.

Kuhn, Thomas S. *The structure of scientific revolutions.* University of Chicago Press; 1970.

Kurzweil, Ray. *The Age of Spiritual Machines.* Penguin Books; 1999.

Kurzweil, Ray. *The Singularity is Near.* Viking; 2005.

Kurzweil, Ray, Grossman, Terry. *Transcend - Nine Steps to Living Well Forever.* Rodale; 2009.

Kurzweil, Ray. *How to Create a Mind - The Secrets of Human Thought Revealed.* Penguin Books; 2012.

Landes, David S. *The Unbound Prometheus: Technological Change and Industrial Development in Western Europe from 1750 to the Present.* Press Syndicate of the University of Cambridge; 1969.

Landes, David S. *The Wealth and Poverty of Nations - Why some are so Rich and Some are so Poor.* WW Norton & Company; 1998.

Liedman, Sven-Eric. *I skuggan av framtiden - Modernitetens idéhistoria.* Albert Bonniers Förlag; 1997.

Lindkvist, Magnus. *Everything We Know is Wrong - The Trendspotter's Handbook.* Marshall Cavendish; 2010.

Lindkvist, Magnus. *The Attack of the Unexpected - A Guide to Surprises and Uncertainty.* Marshall Cavendish; 2011.

Lipsey, Richard G, Carlaw, Kenneth I, Bekar, Clifford T. *Economic Transformations - General Purpose Technologies and Long Term Economic Growth.* Oxford University Press; 2005.

Lipson, Hod, Kurman, Melba. *Fabricated - The New World of 3D Printing.* John Wiley & Sons; 2013.

Lombardo, Thomas. *Contemporary Futurist Thought.* AuthorHouse; 2006.

Lucas, Henry C. *Information Technology and the Productivity Paradox - Assessing the value of Investing in IT.* Oxford University Press; 1999.

Magnusson, Lars, Ottosson, Jan (ed.). *Evolutionary Economics and Path Dependence.* Edward Elgar Publishing; 1997.

Mazarr, Michael J. *Global Trends 2005 - An Owner's Manual for the Next Decade.* Palgrave; 1999.

Mercer, David. *Future Revolutions - Unravelling the Uncertainties of Life and Work in the 21st Century.* Orion Business Books; 1998.

Meyer, Christopher, Davis, Stan. *It's Alive - The Coming Convergence of Information, Biology and Business.* Thomson Texere, 2003.

Miller, James D. S*ingularity Rising – Surviving and Thriving in a Smarter, Richer and More Dangerous World.* BenBella Books; 2012.

Mokyr, Joel. *The Lever of Riches: Technological Creativity and Economic Progress.* Oxford University Press; 1990.

Moore, Geoffrey A. *Inside the Tornado. Harper Business*; 1999.

More, Max, Vita-More, Natasha (Eds). *The Transhumanist Reader.* Wiley-Blackwell; 2013.

Muehlhauser, Luke. Facing the Intelligence Explosion. *Machine Intelligence Research Institute*; 2009.

Nye, David E. *Consuming Power – A Social History of American Energies.* The MIT Press; 1998.

Pearson, Ian. *You Tomorrow. Futurizon Books*; 2011.

Penn, Mark J. Microtrends - *The Small Forces Behind Tomorrow's Big Changes.* Twelve; 2007.

Piore, Michael J, Sabel, Charles F. *The Second Industrial Divide – Possibilities for Prosperity.* Basic Books; 1984.

Pistono, Federico. *Robots Will Steal Your Job But That's OK.* Pistono; 2012.

Ridley, Matt. *The Rational Optimist - How Prosperity Evolves.* Fourth Estate; 2010.

Samuel, Lawrence R. *Future - A Recent History.* University of Texas Press; 2009.

Savulescu, Julian, Bostrom, Nick. *Human Enhancement.* Oxford University Press; 2009.

Sennett, Richard. *The Corrosion of Character – The Personal Consequences of Work in the New Capitalism.* WW Norton & Company; 1998.

Scherer, FM. *New Perspectives on Economic Growth and Technological Innovation.* Brookings Institution Press; 1999.

Schmidt, Eric, Cohen, Jared. *The New Digital Age - Reshaping the Future of People, Nations and Business.* Alfred A Knopf; 2013.

Schumpeter, Joseph A. *Business Cycles: A Theoretical, Historical and Statistical Analysis of the Capitalist Process.* McGraw-Hill; 1939.

Schwartz, Peter. *The Art of the Long View – Planning for the Future in an Uncertain World.* Doubleday; 1996.

Schwartz, Peter, Leyden, Peter, Hyatt, Joel. *The Long Boom – A Vision for the Coming Age of Prosperity.* Perseus Publishing; 1999.

Schwartz, Peter. *Inevitable Surprises - A Survival Guide for the 21st Century.* Simon & Schuster; 2003.

Schön, Lennart. *Industrialismens förutsättningar.* Liber Förlag; 1982.

Silver, Nate. *The Signal and the Noise - Why So Many Predictions Fail, But Some Don't.* The Penguin Press; 2012.

Smith, Laurence C. *The World in 2050 - Four Forces Shaping Civilizations's Northern Future.* Dutton; 2010.

Stearns, Pete. *The industrial revolution in world history.* Westview Press Inc; 1994.

Steiner, Christopher. *Automate This - How Algorithms Came To Rule Our World.* Penguin Books; 2012.

Sturken, Marita, Thomas, Douglas, Ball-Rokeach, Sandra J. *Technological Visions - The Hopes and Fears that Shape New Technologies.* Temple University Press; 2004.

Taleb, Nassim Nicholas. *The Black Swan - The Impact of the Highly Improbable.* Random House; 2007.

Taleb, Nassim Nicholas. *Antifragile - Things That Gain From Disorder.* Random House; 2012.

Tapscott, Don, Caston, Art. *Paradigm Shift.* Harvard Business Press; 1993.

Toffler, Alvin. *The Third Wave.* Pan/Collins; 1981.

Utterback, James. *Mastering the Dynamics of Innovation.* Harvard Business School Press; 1994.

van der Heijden, Kees. *Scenarios - The Art of Strategic Conversation.* John Wiley & Sons; 2005.

Wacker, Watts, Taylor, Jim. *The Visionary's Handbook – Nine Paradoxes That Will Shape the Future of Your Business.* Harper Business; 2000.

Watson, Richard. *Future Files - A Brief History of the Next 50 Years.* Nicholas Brealey Publishing; 2008.

Weiner, Jonathan. *Long for this World - The Strange Science of Immortality.* HarperCollins; 2010.

Åkerman, Johan. *Theory of Industrialism – Casual Analysis and Economic Plans.* Porcupine Press; 1960.

THE
TECHSTORM
PLAYLIST

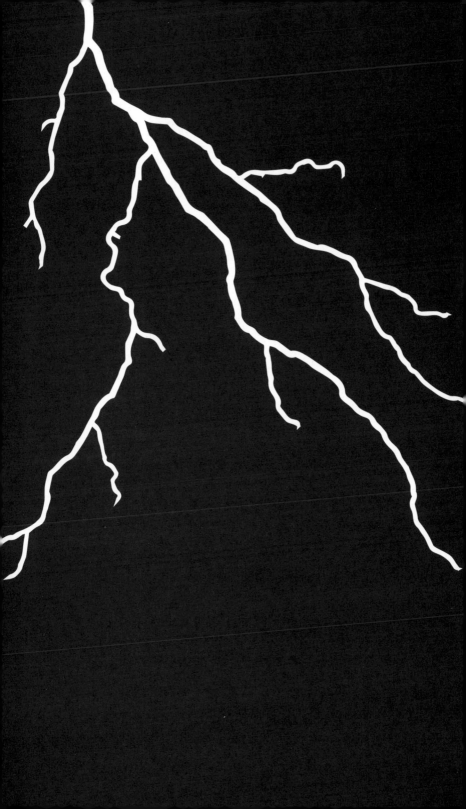

I think and write best when I listen to music, different music depending on where I am in the process. Below is a compilation of the music that was essential for this book project.

The Techstorm Playlist can, of course, be found on Spotify. username: survivingthetechstorm
Enjoy!

Author and Punisher

Band of Horses

Beastie Boys

Bob Hund

Daft Punk

David Bowie

Dr Dre

Esbjörn Svensson Trio

Fläskkvartetten

Frank Zappa

Hansson & Karlsson

The Hellacopters

The Hives

Imperial State Electric

The (International) Noise Conspiracy

Jack Johnson

Jack White

Jason Mraz

King Crimson

The Knife

Kraftwerk

Mando Diao

The Mars Volta

Neighbourhood

Oddjob

Oskar Linnros

Parliament

Phish

Primal Scream

Prominent

Refused

Rollins Band

Samson For President

Shout Out Louds

Silverbullit

Snoop Dogg

The Soundtrack of Our Lives

Stonefunkers

The Strokes

Thelonius Monk

Thomas Rusiak

Thåström

Veronica Maggio

The White Stripes

AN INTRODUCTION TO NICKLAS BERGMAN

Nicklas Bergman spends his days living and breathing high tech, searching for new opportunities arising from the ever-changing technological landscape. As a futurist, he tries to understand where we are heading, and if society will be able to handle the upcoming techstorm.

He is also the Scandinavian advisor to the TechCast Technology Think Tank in Washington DC, working amongst a world-wide network of scientists, policy makers and business executives with the aim of understanding the impact of disruptive technologies.

Through the combination of his entrepreneurial endeavors and technology investments, Nicklas Bergman is uniquely suited to act as a guide to the future of business and technology combined. As a futurist he takes a holistic approach, trying to understand and communicate not only what we might expect from a technological perspective, but also how this possible future and technological development will affect us as individuals, corporations and society as a whole.

www.nicklasbergman.com
www.survivingthetechstorm.com